SUPERnatural Sales Person

By

Dan Maclean

SUPERnatural Salesperson

ISBN- 1537479229

ISBN- 9781537479224
Published by Dan Maclean

Printed in the United States of America.

All Scripture quotations, unless otherwise indicated, are taken from the Holy Bible, New King James version, NKJV, copyright 1982 by Thomas Nelson, Inc. Used by permission. All rights reserved

Scripture quotations marks KJV are taken from the King James Version of the Bible.

Scripture quotations marked "NLT" are taken from the New Living

What Leaders are Saying About Dan Maclean and SUPERnatural Salesperson: The GOD Factor in Sales

"Dan Maclean has written a book that I strongly recommend be given to all managers and sales people. As CEO of a 55-year-old company, I am blessed to have some of the top sales trainers anywhere in the country. Dan has trained many of them. He consistently reminds us that God knows best. The wisdom he's gleaned and teaches from the Word of God has resulted in impacting not only the culture of our company, but consistent year after year growth. Every once in a while, a book comes along that is a game changer."

The **SUPER**natural Salesperson; The **GOD** Factor in Sales, is a book that's time has come."

Chris Adamson
CEO
National Write Your Congressman, Inc.

"I thought I was a highly skilled selling professional and then I met Dan Maclean. Fifteen years ago, our paths crossed. He became my mentor, coach and friend helping me discover my true purpose and God-given calling in this world. The principles you will learn in this book will profoundly impact every aspect of your life bringing your head, heart and soul into alignment. You will walk in peace and serve without fear! Dan Maclean can help you unlock the door to your birthright of prosperity, peace and love through serving others in this most noble of professions."

Chris Allen
President, CEO
ICCS, Inc.

"Dan has a gift that few people have; he can teach, train, and motivate. He has a unique ability to connect with people and by doing so, he can coach and develop people through trust and the fact that he can demonstrate success. I have had the privilege of being trained by Dan and as a former National Director of training, I was blown away by his talents.
The concepts in this book are not ethereal nor theoretical. They are practical, powerful and written by someone who is in the field developing top producers."

George Oubre
Former National Training Director of N.F.I.B.
(National Federation of Independent Business)

"I've had the privilege of working with Dan Maclean over the last eighteen years. In all those years, I have watched as he has intentionally pursued the mind and will of Christ in his work. As a sales leader and trainer, Dan has a way of connecting Biblical truths and Spirit-filled insights to his career that yield exponential results. He is consistently reminding us that we are looking for the "God idea" not the "good idea". Dan's writings are filled with "God ideas" that lead and guide us toward His preferred future for each of us."

Mark Wade
Regional Sales Manager
and National Training Director
National Write Your Congressman, Inc.

"Dan is the consummate sales professional. His experience and gift for communicating has added value to my professional career for more than a decade. More importantly, his focus on Biblical principles is not just refreshing, it's what makes his instruction so meaningful."
Richard Wells
President
Live Well Solutions

Dedications:

I am proud to dedicate this book to my beautiful wife of almost 40 years, Judi; our two wonderful daughters, Nicole and Dara; and their husbands, Zac and Donnie; our grandbabies Payton and Dean; and to my Dad, Dan, and my step mother, Norma.

▲ ▲ ▲

To Judi: Not only are you beautiful, but you are the picture of a virtuous woman. You see me the way God does, even in my off days. Your love for me, our family and others inspires us all. I'm looking forward to spending an eternity with you. Love you forever.

▲ ▲ ▲

To Nicole: You are the picture of class. In the business world, you bring God's heart to those you oversee. Your love for me and your faith in me makes me want to be a better father and leader. I love you and am more proud of you than words can say.

▲ ▲ ▲

To Dara: You are carrying His heart to the world in music and message. I've watched you mature into a woman of God whose singular desire is to know Him and make Him known. Thank you (and Donnie) for nudging me to write, get this book out and to change the cover design! Love you, daughter.

To Zac: My fireman son-in-law. You impact lives on a level few realize. Thank you for your love for my daughter and being "Father of the Year" to Payton and Dean. I also, want to thank you for your respect for me. I appreciate you more than I've been able to tell you. Love you.

▲ ▲ ▲

To Donnie: My preacher son-in-law. You are revealing His heart and impacting lives for His kingdom. When our daughter fell in love with you, the whole family did as well. Thank you for your wisdom regarding this project. Love you.

▲ ▲ ▲

To Dad: Thank you, Dad. You've always encouraged me to do things even when I didn't know if I could. Thank you for your wisdom. I find myself thinking many times of the things you've told me and realize, "That was a "Dadism!" You have said, tongue in cheek, I haven't given you credit. I am now. I love you.

▲ ▲ ▲

To Norma: Norm, you are amazing (and not just in how you cook. Thank you for loving us the way God does and for seeing us with His eyes. I admire your strength and compassion through some very challenging trials. I love you.

Contents

Introduction

By Dan Maclean

There is a psychological concept called determinism that says we're limited by certain factors like natural talent, gifting, ability etc. In our attempt to break out of these limitations, we're off to the races on a new self-improvement plan. The containment we experience however, is our mental real estate has borders of noble intentions which include trying our hardest to be our best. The truth of the matter is, these noble intentions represent ceilings that contain us from being all God's created us to be.

This book is not about YOUR limits or the human potential and it is certainly not your typical book about sales. Being all you can be is not all there is! In fact, your best or worst for that matter, are no longer the point. Discovering your DNA as a child of God is. I am not going to encourage you to pull yourself up by your bootstraps. I am going to show you from God's Word how He wants you to do beyond what you can "naturally" do.

There are laws governing flight that have always existed, but until they were understood, humanity was grounded. Once they were discovered and leveraged, they became the foundation for achieving flight.

We too have often been grounded by not having a knowledge or vision for God's way of doing things. For example, where do most people go to learn sales? There are a plethora of self-help books on the subject and some have excellent principles. I will and do study some of these books. However, the truth is, the best source of teaching and the greatest Book written about sales or life for that matter, is the same today same as it has been for thousands of years; the Bible. It is the litmus test for all truth.

The paradigm you discover in the Bible isn't about being the best you can be. This may be the road you've attempted to take most, but there is another path and that is being who He's created you to be. As this truth dawns on you, your next step can be in the energy and power of God. This isn't a Sunday morning sermon that has no reality Monday morning. What I'm going to share with you, I've experienced and taught for over 20 years. It is more than a religious concept, more than an ethic, and something more than the philosophy of a sentimental idealist without power. It is this something, which makes it relevant to each one of us right now in our sales careers, in our businesses, in our parenting, in every human endeavor.

I've been married close to 40 years. Knowing Him and discovering his way of doing things has made be a better husband.

I have two children, knowing Him has made me a better Father.

I am in business and ministry, all of which I do from a place of purposing to know Him and His ways.

In one of my business roles I'm a National Sales Trainer. According to the CEO of a major fifty-five year old company, I have trained more six figure earners than anyone else. Not from a distance, but in the field where the rubber meets the road. Everything I've done and taught, I've learned from doing business by "THE BOOK."

Before I knew the Lord, my journey in sales started out somewhat jaded. I thought sales was something you did to a person not for them. I would go from one job to another, looking for a better paying more appealing job. The problem is, I took myself with me.

When I came to know Him, he gave me a know-how and everything changed. He taught me from His Word, how to do it right and then how to do it empowered.

God has "pre-determined" for us not to be limited by what we can do but what He can do through us.

Learning to be dependent on God will make you independent from the pressure of circumstances and freed from a self-oriented paradigm which, on the one hand causes you to be arrogant or on the other hand, causes you to wallow in self-pity. This is a new paradigm which accesses His power.

We've been satisfied with the human potential instead of the God potential and as a result, we never achieve real sustained purpose, passion or empowerment. We've settled for the superficial instead of the supernatural. I believe, it's time to see God at work in and through us where He puts His SUPER on our natural!

Chapter 1
The SUPERnatural Salesperson:
The GOD Factor in Sales

Being the Best GOD Has Created You to Be

Those who trust in the Lord will find new strength. They will soar high on wings like eagles. They will run and not grow weary. They will walk and not faint: Isaiah 40:31 NLT

The Pretoria Zoo is the largest zoo in South Africa. This zoo is home to over 8,000 different animals, reptiles, fish and birds-- one of which was a black eagle. After 10 years in a cage, the head Zoo keeper decided it was time to free this bird to return to the life of its design. However, excitement soon turned to frustration when, after the cage was opened, the bird refused to fly! Ten years of caged life trapped this magnificent creature in an invisible enclosure. No amount of prodding or prompting helped. After several hours, the bird caught a glimpse and then gazed at another eagle that was soaring. Suddenly, as though a light went on, the eagle took off in flight! What does an Eagle do to earn their wings? Nothing but being born an Eagle. No flying lessons are required when truth dawns on us!

How many of us have been contained by what we can naturally do?

Our ceiling is a "self" manufactured one. We've been contained by what is reasonable to our abilities not realizing that God wants us to function at a different level. Jesus did not come to upgrade the cage of "self" but to reveal the new creation and redeem the image of God in us! His mission was to reveal our original design, not as an example for us but of us! (Col 1:15, 2:9, 10). He came to set us free from who we used to be so He can put His SUPER on our natural.

I wanted to write a book about sales that was profoundly different than what has been written in the past. The difference is the fact that we don't have to be limited to relying on our self. We can draw from the limitless SUPERnatural resource God provides by learning to rely on Him.

As a national sales trainer, I've mentored, coached and developed some of the top sales producers in the country. The message taught in this book is not an ethereal concept that has no use on Monday morning where life happens. I've taught and continue to teach these truths in the field where, as a trainer, I'm forced to by-pass theory and get results. I've been in sales for years and have discovered that many self-help books have valuable ideas if they are processed correctly.

For starters, every principle I learn, I process through the Word of God because the Bible is the acid test for all truth. Just as important, when we're talking about being empowered, self is not the center or the source. Christ is! When you're not connecting and processing these principles through a knowledge of Him, you'll find yourself in the box (or cage) of being the best you can be rather than the best God, your Father, has created you to be.

What I'm going to share with you has given me and those I've trained, new levels of passion, purpose and empowerment.

This book will not resonate with those who believe they have all the answers. A key to grasping these truths is humility which gives us the ability to get past ourselves and discover the Greater One in us. The professional that thinks skill and technique are the end all and be all won't grasp these concepts. This book is for those who realize there is something deeper and more profound available to them than just "self-help." Your heart knows it! The Bible says: He has given us a heart to know HIM (Jer 24:7). Substitutes won't satisfy.

I often tell people that Father knows best and He definitely knows sales. It never ceases to amaze me how concepts from His Word are profoundly applicable in the field.

Unlike any other profession except maybe politicians and lawyers, sales people get a bad rap.

Unfortunately, there are times it is well deserved.

Yet when done His way, selling is a noble profession. At the same time, what I'm talking about is a choice to go beyond a profession and on to a "Higher" calling.

You may be surprised to learn that the Old English word for sales originally meant "to give!" This has the Golden Rule written all over it. Today, though, for many, the original meaning has morphed into a new meaning, "to get!" When we learn God's perspective, we will not only learn how to be on the give, but we'll go beyond the natural and experience the SUPERnatural.

Jesus laid out the pathway we're to follow, not just in our careers, but in life when He said, *"You must be born again."(Jn 3:7) This is foundational, so let me briefly explain. In the manufacturers' handbook called the Bible, God reveals that, as humans, we are created in three parts: spirit, soul and body (1 Thess 5:23). When Adam fell, the whole of humanity fell; death came to man's spirit. We lost the capacity to truly love or live without a self-centered perspective. Principles you discover in "self-help" books, as long as they line up with the Word of God, can be very helpful. At the same time, they are not the ultimate remedy for what ails or challenges humanity. Like one person put it, "The problems of life cannot be remedied on the same level they were created." This is why Jesus said we must be born again (i.e. our spirits) and that happens by receiving Him (See Note below).

Our soul, which is comprised of our mind, will and emotions is a work in progress. The change that takes place the moment we accept Christ affects our spirit immediately. Then it is up to us to renew our minds with the Word of God so that what is now true in our spirits becomes true in our thinking and becomes visible to our world (Rom 12:2).

I said all of that to say this, being born again now qualifies you to impact people at an entirely different level. Your capacity to truly love, be on the give, and influence people for the right reasons becomes as natural as breathing, yet it has a supernatural element to it. As a new creation in Christ, you can draw from new resources. Maturing in these "new creation" realities, you will discover what it means not just to have your head into what you're doing, but also, truly, your heart. You will discover new levels of Professionalism, Passion and Purpose, all the while empowered to do more in less time with less stress.

You might ask, "How can you make such promises?" I can because I have God's Word on it and I've experienced precisely what I'm preaching. I've been able to share and teach these concepts to others and have seen them become top producers and set records.

This is God's version of the sales profession, which when done His way, becomes a calling. In this book you'll discover the practical and the powerful.

Topics we'll discuss include vision, purpose, and influence, all the while being empowered in the most wonderful journey you can embark upon: To know Him. Know Him, know how. No Him, No way.

NOTE: *If you haven't received Jesus as Savior, what are you waiting for? See a simple prayer at the end of this book.*

Chapter 2
Know Him:

The Key to the SUPERnatural

Proverbs 3:6 says we are to acknowledge Him, in all our ways and He will direct our path. The Maclean Monday a.m. user-friendly version of that Scripture is, Know Him in what you do, and He'll show you the HOW to and give you the POWER to!

To go beyond what we can naturally do, we must have a vision for it. The key to supernatural living and (selling) is the revelation of Christ in us.

I told you this was not going to be a book about sales as usual.

The Bible says, Greater is He in us (1Jn 4:4). This is the powerful reality of the New Creation. Any man who is in Christ is a new creation. The old (version of him) has passed and the new (version) is come (i.e. who he is in Christ) and the new is of God (2Cor 5:17)! To be empowered, there needs to be an exchange. We must put off the old and then by faith, put on the new (Eph 4:22-24).

If we're really relating to God in truth (and not according to the traditions of men), and if we want to experience success in our career and in life, we must have a greater awareness and revelation of Him alive in us.

Without this revelation, we will continue to gravitate toward being self-reliant, rather than putting our trust in Him. Those who focus on the worst or best they have been apart from Christ are just in a different size box.

The key to breaking out of whatever box you are in is to learn to focus on Him. How? Renew your mind by thinking about and meditating on the "in Him" Scriptures. As you do, His Word will begin to resonate within you and you will notice a changing of gears.

Your true identity is who God has created you to be in Christ. There are over 100 Scriptures in the New Testament that talk about being "in Christ", Christ in us, "in whom", etc.

When our thinking is renewed with these new creation realities, we begin to discover the God gear. As we receive Him, He gives us the power to live life. (See Jn 1:12-13) It is not will power or limited by natural talent nor does it originate with us. It is of God. Here are some examples of new creations realities in Christ:

2Corinthians 5:17-18 Therefore, if anyone is in Christ, he is a new creation; old things have passed away; behold, all things have become new. Now all things (the new things) are of God...

Empowering Application: If you find yourself limited by who you used to be, i.e. your old habits, hang-ups or limitations, etc., or even if you are self-confident, but know there's something more, change your thinking. Consider this, in Christ, you are a new creation. Christianity is not a sentimental philosophy without power. Neither is it a "self" improvement plan. This journey is not meant to help you discover a new improved version of who you used to be. The journey each of us is on is to KNOW Him and experience a new life with new resources. This is a powerful truth. It reframes our world and reveals that, "in Christ" we have God's DNA. The world doesn't need us to play small ball by being all we can be-naturally speaking. Instead, we need to tap into His bottomless truth and the limitless resources of who God has created us to be. When you step out by faith relying on Him and not leaning on yourself, He will empower you to do life as well as your career at levels of purpose, passion, empowerment and fulfillment, you never dreamed possible. Renewing your mind is the key.

Romans 1:16 says, "I am not ashamed of the Gospel of Christ, for it (i.e. the Gospel of Christ) is the power of God to everyone who believes!"

Romans 8:2 For the law of the Spirit of life in Christ Jesus has made me free from the law of sin and death.

Empowering Application: This law of the Spirit of life in Christ overrides the law of who you used to be. This is irrefutable, undeniable and unstoppable if you keep your focus on Him.

1 Corinthians 15:22 For as in Adam all die, even so in Christ all shall be made alive.

Empowering Application: In Adam, again, is who you used to be. Dying is not just talking about the end of your days; it is about not being truly alive while you're living. All the while being limited by what you can or cannot do in your natural strength. As you become aware of Christ in you, you draw from the limitlessness of His resources and ability.

2 Corinthians 1:21 Now He who establishes us with you in Christ and has anointed us is God.

Empowering Application: From God our Father, comes security and identity so we can walk out our destiny in His ability. The anointing is God's ability to do through us what we cannot do apart from Him.

HIS SUPER on our natural. If we get this, it will get us! Why live superficially when you can live supernaturally?

2 Corinthians 2:14 Now thanks be to God who always leads us in triumph in Christ, and through us diffuses the fragrance of His knowledge in every place.

Empowering Application: The knowledge of Him is true power and how we live as victors not victims in life. All failure is "self" inflicted. When we learn to lean on, expect, and trust Christ, we find what true success is. This knowledge affects everything we are and everything we do.

Ephesians 1:3 Blessed be the God and Father of our Lord Jesus Christ, who has blessed us with every spiritual blessing in the heavenly places in Christ.

Empowering Application: Some think, "I just can't, I don't have, I never was, I never will be." On the other side of the coin, some think, "I've arrived, I'm all that and a bag of chips!" We're talking about a new frame of reference. We must renew our minds and humbly replace those thought with who God says we are. He has equipped us with all things we need to overcome any challenges we face and to experience what it means to be truly blessed in the process.

Ephesians 2:10 For we are His workmanship, created in Christ Jesus for good works, which God prepared beforehand that we should walk in them.

Empowering Application: Yes, Dan, I hear you, but what does that have to do with sales? Did you know God want His kids to shine in their sphere of influence? We need to learn how to wear Jesus in the market place.

Ministry is not just someone behind a pulpit preaching a sermon. We are in the "calling" of sales and we need to bring the knowledge of Him to what we do. These powerful truths are not for the sweet by and by but, for the challenging here and now.

Philippians 4:13 I can do all things through Christ who strengthens me.

Empowering Application: "Just do it" takes on a whole new meaning when it dawns on us, In Him I can do all things!

When I began to believe "this" (Christ in me) and not "that" (who I used to be or what I could do apart from Him), I realized I can do this business and life at another level because it's Him in me doing what I'm called to do through me.

Here are some additional empowering thoughts about our identity in Christ.... (i.e. In Him, In Christ, etc.)

- **In Christ**, I reign in life (i.e. I'm not under it...I've over it (Rom. 5:17).

- I walk in newness of life (Rom. 6:4).

- I am truly alive (Rom. 6:11).

- I have no condemnation (Rom. 8:1).

- I am a child of God (Rom. 8:16).

- I am an heir of God (Rom. 8:17).

- I am a joint-heir with Christ (Rom. 8:17).

- I freely receive all things from God (Rom. 8:32).

- I am more than a conqueror (Rom. 8:37).

- **In Christ**, nothing can separate me from the love of God (Rom. 8:38-39).

- I am sanctified (set apart) (1 Cor. 1:2).

- I am enriched in all knowledge (1 Cor. 1:5).

- I have wisdom (1 Cor. 1:30).

- I have righteousness-(no sense of inferiority, or not belonging to God) (1 Cor. 1:30).

- I have redemption-(forgiveness) (1 Cor. 1:30).

- I shall be resurrected (i.e. I have eternal life) (1 Cor. 15:20-22).

- I have victory (1 Cor. 15:57).

- All the promises of God to me are "Yes" and "Amen" (i.e. so be it) (2 Cor. 1:20).

- I am established (secure) (2 Cor. 1:21).

- I am anointed of God (i.e. I have an ability beyond my own) (2 Cor. 1:21).

- I always triumph (2 Cor. 2:14).

- My mind is renewed and enlightened (2 Cor. 3:14).

- I am a new creation (2 Cor. 5:17).

- **In Christ**, I am an ambassador for God (2 Cor. 5:20).

- I am made the righteousness of God (2 Cor. 5:21).

- I live by the power of God (2 Cor. 13:4).

- I have liberty (Gal. 2:4).

- I am redeemed from the curse (no longer struggling, but blessed) (Gal. 3:13).

- I am a son of God (Gal. 4:7).

- I have faith which works by love (Gal. 5:6).

- I am blessed (Eph. 1:3).

- I have been chosen (Eph. 1:4).

- I am accepted (highly favored) of God (Eph. 1:6). I am His workmanship (Eph. 2:10).

- I am created for good works (Eph. 2:10).

- I am built together for a habitation of God through the Spirit (I didn't say this, God did...He dwells in us by His Spirit, just sayin' (Eph. 2:22)

- I have boldness and access with confidence towards God (Eph. 3:12).

- **In Christ**, I am a shining light (Eph. 5:8).

- I am strong in the power of God's might (Eph. 6:10).

- I have the high calling of God (changes your career into a calling) (Phil. 3:14).

- I do not worry (Phil 4:6).

- I have the peace of God which passes all understanding (Phil. 4:7).

- **In Christ**, I have strength and I can do all things (Phil. 4:13).

- All my needs are met (Phil. 4:19).

- I have been delivered from the power of darkness (Col. 1:13).

- I have forgiveness (Col. 1:14).

- I am reconciled to God (Col. 1:20).

- I have all the treasures of wisdom and knowledge (Col. 2:3).

- I am made complete and perfect (Col. 2:10).

- **In Christ**, I have joy unspeakable (1 Peter 1:8).

- I have received the anointing which teaches me all things (1 John 2:27).

- I have the Spirit of God (1 John 3:24).

- I have overcome (1 John 4:4).

- I have no fear (1 John 4:18).

- I have victory (1 John 5:4).

- I have understanding (1 John 5:20).

- I know God (1 John 5:20).

For other Scriptures, refer to this website:

In Him, In Whom, In Christ Scriptures

https://www.scribd.com/doc/8081207

As you meditate on these Scriptures (i.e. think, pray, say, step out on these realities), you will find a power beyond your own. You will experience first-hand, that by renewing your mind with these "exceedingly great and precious promises," you are becoming a partaker of His divine nature (2Pet 1:3).

From now on, you and your world will never be the same. All the while you will give honor to God, your Father.

Chapter 3:

A Matter of Perspective

A Purpose Driven Life

God, our Father, has a purpose for us that is not only wonderful, but it works because it is the way we're wired!

He has gifted us and called us to impact our world, and to show that in whatever we are called to do, He knows best. I'm in the profession of sales, which when I began to understand God's purpose, I realized he wanted me to influence people in the industry to look to Him for the what, why and how. This has elevated my training/coaching/mentoring career to a calling with purpose written all over it. Some think the only calling by God is to the pulpit ministry. I would say, there are a whole lot of Pastors who should be influencing and impacting lives in the market place. There are some sales people who should be Pastors, but a whole lot less. Ministry happens whenever purpose is clear. To me, there is no difference between the secular and sacred because my purpose is to know Him in all I do. Proverbs 3:6 (Amp.) says, "In all your ways know, recognize, and acknowledge Him, and He will direct and make straight and plain your paths."

If you're called to be a Pastor or whatever you are called to do, what you learn here will help equip you.

The calling on all of us is to know Him which means to learn to draw from His wisdom, His ability, His motives in what we do and then we are called to make Him known! When this becomes our determined purpose, He will show us the "rest" of the story!

Second Timothy 1:9 says, "Who has saved us and called us with a holy calling, not according to our works, but according to His own purpose and grace which was given to us in Christ Jesus before time began." We find our purpose in knowing Him. We also lose sight of purpose when we lose sight of Him. A popular coffee shop posted this saying on a billboard, "Pencil yourself in everywhere." Wrong answer! Apart from Him, we can do nothing (Jn 15:5) including discover the purpose He's called us to.

I remember a story about a young woman who won a gold medal in the Olympics. She was in tears. Many thought they were tears of joy, and why not? She had accomplished not only what very few have but, what she'd always dreamed about. The truth is, when she reached this pinnacle of success, she silently asked herself, "Is this all there is?" Maybe, you have asked yourself the same question. The "Tombstone" test is a good way to examine our perspective. When we draw our last breath, what do we want our tombstone to read? Here lies (Insert your name). He made a lot of sales and broke a lot of records in the process! Or, Here lies ....., He not only broke a lot of sales records, but he impacted a lot of lives for good and for God! David understood this when he said, "Lord, teach me to number my days that I may be wise in the end!"

This message is about perspective and finding new levels of purpose, passion and empowerment. The epiphany for me has been that whether it's the people I train or the potential customers I meet, I'm impacting lives for His sake. This journey is not about a psychological way of approaching a career or simply positive thinking. It is about the sustaining power, purpose, and passion discovered at the heart level and revealed by God, our Father, in Christ.

Chapter 4

How do you see you?

More Importantly, How Does God See You?

How we see ourselves determines how productive we are. We can't see ourselves as victims and behave as victors. We can't see ourselves as overwhelmed and be the overcomers we have been created in Christ to be.

At the same time, the way we see ourselves can be skewed if we don't know the way God, our Father, sees us. When I know His thoughts toward me and His value of me, I can impact my world. Psalm 139 is just one of many Psalms that reveals His heart. He knows us best and loves us most. The "rest" of the story? Only His opinion matters! Call reluctance or the sense of rejection can be swallowed up whenever this dawns on you. When you know and believe His love, fear is cast out (1Jn 4:18)!

God thinks about us 24/7 and those thoughts are precious (Ps 139:17). He's not put out with us. He loves us through the ups and downs of life and when we know that, we accept His invitation to come to Him without reservation. Knowing He welcomes us on our good or bad days, we have fewer bad days.

David was affected by this truth when he said, "Surely (His) goodness and mercy shall follow me all the days of my life!" (Ps 23:6) "All the days" means exactly that, on our good or bad days. Understanding this powerful truth even if we fall, we'll learn to fall forward, fall less, and get up fast. Just as importantly, we'll discover how to draw from His strength, ability, and wisdom. We'll do more in less time, enjoy what we do and find we are functioning SUPERnaturally. We will do more than we can do!

Psalm 100 wasn't a psalm attributed to David, but it was on his playlist. It starts out by saying shout out to God, serve Him with joy!

What is the source of such inspiration? Why was David so excited?

I suggest if we get this, it will get us. He says in verse 3, "Know this, it is God who has made us and not we ourselves!" We're God-made, not self-made, and God doesn't make junk.

It dawned on David that God created him and he was up to any challenge he faced. If we know God has made us, we don't have to be contained in the box of who we used to be—good or bad. We are a new creation in Christ. The old is gone. The new is come and the new is of God. In Christ, we have God's DNA. We need to act like it is so and God will honor it. None of this happens outside-in. It must be inside-out. This is the key to not only supernatural selling, but supernatural living!

Chapter 5
Power in the Right Paradigm

Without a redemptive revelation (A vision), we cast off restraint, but happy is he who does the Word. A servant may hear, but not be able to respond. (Prov 29:18-19) Personal Paraphrase.

A well-known minister passed by a tattoo studio as he was walking through the twisted little streets of Kowloon, Hong Kong.

In the window were various examples of tattoos.

You could have a tattooed anchor or flag or mermaid or whatever, on the chest or arms.

He was struck by one tattoo of three words: "Born to lose."

Amazed, he asked the Chinese tattoo artist, "Does anyone really have that phrase, Born to lose, tattooed on his body?"

The tattoo artist replied, "Yes, sometimes."

"But," the minister said, "I just can't believe that anyone in his right mind would do that."

The Chinese man simply tapped his forehead and said in broken English, "Before tattoo on body, tattoo on mind."

We might have a positive spin, and have "Born to win" tattooed on our mind, but, the power I am talking about is not limited by your best nor obviously your worst. Both are based on what you can do, but Christ said, apart from Him, you can do nothing.

Many books about sales are about being the best you can be. God wants you to tap into the limitlessness of who He's created you to be. Only as a believer with vision can you tap into a level of passion, purpose, and power that God intended. We are not limited to what WE can do about it.

We can run faster than we can run. We can do more than we can do. In fact, the statement, "I can only do what I can do" is not applicable to a child of God when this truth dawns on them. We are to draw from a deeper well than the best we can be, and we don't have to be limited by the worst we have been. Instead, we are drawing from a new paradigm that is Christ in us. Paul said Christ in us is a mystery (Col 1:27). I might add, it isn't a mystery hidden from us. It is hidden for us. Self-reliance is to be replaced by reliance on Christ, the greater one in us. Self-image and esteem are discovered in Him. He is to be the centerpiece of the "new creation" masterpiece.

We have value in Him. Our image is an "in-Him" image that changes everything. Our journey then becomes one of knowing Him, and, as you do, you will make Him known. Those who are struggling will come to you.

Even those who are, in the world's terms, successful, will see that you're not just about numbers; you're doing that, but you're about much more. You are living a purpose-driven life with God's SUPER on your natural. You can only run with what you have a vision of—what is tattooed on your mind, if you will. The message in this book is meant to open your eyes so you can run with a vision of something beyond yourself. Throw the record books out because you are not going to achieve what you had believed is the best you can do. You are not going from good to great. Instead, you are going to experience what it means to be Godly as HE gives you wisdom to do your career and life His way. When you do, you will bring a different level of performance as you access the God factor!

Chapter 6
True North - True Power

True north is a navigational term referring to the direction of the North Pole relative to a navigator's position. It is about orientation.

When we use it in the context of our lives, it is the internal compass that guides us successfully through life so we don't become disoriented in our thinking or decision making. True North for a Christian represents who we are in Christ and how we function from core level conviction and motivation.

When we are aligned with who God says we are and we seek His way of doing things, we will find we live a life that is purposeful, meaningful, and empowered. Until then, we are like ships at sea without a compass or rudder.

The business world is discovering there is something deeper and more impactful than self-interest. There are many books being written on this profound Biblical truth. *True North* is one of those books that explores this topic.

Successful CEOs of major corporations were interviewed.

The common denominator of these very successful people: not one of them made money the priority. They know profit is important but their internal compass was mission, not money. Very simply put, they discovered the "why" and then an interesting thing happened—they became very successful monetarily, and, I might add, very satisfied. By the way, if you have to apologize for prosperity, you will have to apologize for what the Bible says is the principal thing, WISDOM. "Wisdom offers long life as well as wealth and honor." (Prov 3:16 Good News Translation) God delights in prospering us (Deut 30:9) which means a whole lot more than money, but it certainly does not exclude it. He is not opposed to blessing us monetarily; He's opposed to us putting money first. His way is to put giving and blessing others first! When we do, we'll be blessed in what we do; doing it our way, not so much!

In another book entitled Firms of Endearment, it was discovered that companies that adopt this internal-compass culture are blowing away the S&P averages. They have true north core values that seek to maximize their value to society as a whole by focusing on the needs of the customer first, and not just the shareholders. The result is a greater service to the customer and greater earnings for shareholders. The world of Commerce is finding out God's principles are the best practices.

Businesses that have defined success in terms that are more about mission than money have discovered money follows. This is the golden rule found in the Bible.

In Matt. 6:33 (Amp) gives us a key principle to live by... Seek first the kingdom of God and His ways of doing and being right and all these things shall be added to you. The "things" are what others stress as a priority (i.e. money, gain, etc.) before God's principles.

Prov. 4:7 says that wisdom is the principal thing. It must be sought after as a priority. It is how we make right decisions, and how we do what we do for the right reasons. As we purpose to embrace wisdom, we find out how to be a blessing and in return we're blessed. It is how we can have a long-term career as well as a fulfilled life.

Being selfless about our approach to life--where we're focused on what's important to others--is not a destination. It is a daily discovery of who we are in Christ. Our core convictions then become a powerful influence. People are moved by what moves us.

I have trained several people who have hit the proverbial wall which can be best described as a crisis of conviction. You can be professional but lose your passion and become a peddler.

Without a sense of a transcendent purpose on the job (i.e., to be on the give)-we're reduced to doing things for the wrong reasons.

Whether it is for ego's sake, selfish interest, or just to make a buck, this kind of "shallow Hal" thinking has short legs. It may work in a sprint, but not in the marathon we call life.

These values form the basis of your personal true north. The result is you make tangible in experience what the Bible says you are by promise. A clear understanding of who you are and your values, from God's point of view, will create the boundaries for your actions.

Our Christianity becomes real and more than a bumper sticker when we go through the transformation process of placing ME first to placing others first. As you learn this, the levels of purpose, passion and empowerment will increase exponentially.

Chapter 7 The Ultimate Attitude and Aptitude Adjustment

The Bible has a lot to say about this topic. In fact, if we're in Christ, God has said that we are a new creation. The old has passed and the new has taken its place, and, as we mentioned before, the new is of God. That little word, "of," speaks volumes. It tells us that when we're born again, we have a new nature. We have new resources to draw from. We're not who we were. When you choose HIM, you are a new you! Our performance or lack thereof cannot convince God that we are anything other than who He says we are. That's why, when we mess up, we need to fess up and then, by faith in Christ, get up. This is how we grow up! We don't need to be stuck in the old. What we need is to renew our minds to what He says about us because He's not budging! Aren't you glad? He has given us His Word and by it we are partakers of His divine nature. Yes, that's in the BIBLE: 2 Pet. 1:4. In other words, when you have accepted Christ you have a supernatural nature. You have been made a child of God. Your identity is not an improved version of who you were; it is an entirely new "in-Him image". Your value is based on being in Christ. You have His righteousness, (i.e. His right standing) before God. You are loved with the same love the Father has for the Son!

If you get this, it will get you and everything changes: Your work becomes a calling and you don't just show up; you know, you are sent. Like the Blues Brothers sarcastically said, "We're on a mission from God." I believe that. We're an answer to prayer. We're on kingdom business. Talk about an attitude and aptitude adjustment!

To progress to the next level in our calling we must put off the old man and put on the new! (Eph 4:22-24)

God didn't send Jesus so we could enter a self-improvement program. We're not a renovation or a remodeling project. The born-again experience is not an extreme makeover of the old. We are a new creation!

We have a new paradigm, new resources, new abilities, and a new well to draw from if we will just learn to get comfortable in our born-again skin by renewing our minds with the Word of God!

But, if we don't renew our minds, we'll function from who we were BC—before Christ—and that is limited and lifeless.

The Old Testament is 1/3 prophetic in nature. It foretold of how Christ would come, live, die and rise again. The reason I came to Christ was I began to study these prophesies and was amazed to discover, I am not serving a man-made God who is still in the grave.

I received another, even more profound, aha moment came when I realized He's alive and wants to live life through me. I don't have the limits of what "I" can do about life apart from Him because I am not apart from Him and neither are you. He is with us, for us and in us! All of what I said is in your Bible. At the same time, even in the Old Testament, before the born-again experience, people would break out of the mold of men's opinions, find what God said about them, and by trusting Him, impact their generation. Jabez, whose name meant one who brings pain, is a powerful example. His name was a reminder of all the heartache caused by the fall of man and the accompanying curse. Now, if the world names you, that's one thing. But, it was his mom who named him! I mean moms will find something good in you even if you just robbed a bank! Every time someone called Jabez' name, they were basically saying, "Here comes the one who brings pain!" In that culture, in those times, names defined you. The cruelty and containment of others' opinions who snickered when they used his name, could have caused Jabez to be a victim. BUT, GOD!!!!

Jabez boldly asked God to bless him and to expand his territory, which, in those days, also meant to expand his influence.

What does this example have to do with sales?

Remember, we are applying powerful principles from the manufacturer's handbook and not from a self-help book!

In our terms, when you have expanded influence you are making sales at an altogether different level.

Jabez found that as he trusted God, he got out of the box of people's opinions and as a result, his life brought blessings and not pain. The Bible God honored him above his brethren. Some who have been indoctrinated by man-made religious thinking might say: "Jabez, who do you think you are?" I believe his answer would be: "It's not about who I think I am, but who God says I am!" This is true humility!

You see, what God says about us must be taken by faith. Jabez knew God's heart and by faith took His promise. This is how we're going to have an impact for God and for good in our world. If we're going to embrace what we do as a calling, we're going to have to renew our minds to who we are!

This is not psychological, nor is it merely semantics. It is the power of the Gospel.

Our self-concept affects our attitude and our aptitude.

All of us look at life in different ways.

Romans 12: 2 offers a revolutionary concept available to us.

It says, "Be not conformed to this world, but be transformed by the renewing of your mind!" The word "transformed" comes from the Greek word for metamorphosis. God, our Father, uses the canvas of creation to illustrate the truth He is wanting to teach us.

For example, a lowly caterpillar crawls on its belly but then morphs into a magnificent butterfly. What a picture of a supernatural transformation! The lesson for us? We don't have to crawl around in what we can do naturally. He has called us and created us to the SUPERnatural. We must renew our minds and get a vision for it, but make no mistake, the greatest attitude and aptitude adjustment is when we renew our minds and begin to think about ourselves the way God thinks about us.

It is then that our lives take on a new level of effectiveness, influence and empowerment. I'm for that, how about you?

Chapter 8 Faith that Accesses the SUPERnatural

Life, I mean truly living, is a faith journey.

Faith trusts what God says and begins to say it, think it and act like it's so. However, have you noticed that God's thoughts do not track with the world's way of thinking? In fact, the natural mind fights God's realities with human reasoning (Rom 8:7).

When we're thinking wrong (all of us have been guilty, we follow this way of believing: If it feels like it or looks like it, I believe.

Yet when we are in faith according to the Bible, we believe because of what God says in His Word.

The victory we possess during our day is another step of faith. God, in the context of faith, told Joshua, everyplace you step, I have given it to you (Josh 1:3). Faith, is our connection to the SUPERnatural. It takes steps; it doesn't stay home.

I don't want to sound like Captain Obvious here, but I'm not talking about faith in ourselves. Our usual default mechanism is to try harder, be our best, give it all we've got, etc. and though that sounds good, it is actually a misplaced faith in what we can "naturally" do about it. To act right, we must believe right and that involves replacing trust in ourselves with trust in Him.

How? Romans 10:17 says, "Faith comes by hearing, hearing the Word of God." The repetition in this verse of "hearing" is important because it speaks of a lifestyle. In addition, our faith becomes effective and powerful as we center on Christ and acknowledge every good thing we have in Him (Philemon 1:6).

Our breakthrough to stellar results happens as we take another step of faith in that context. The pressure we feel to perform is replaced by the power of God to perform. I've seen this happen time and time again. When the day doesn't "look" like it's working out, I take another step of faith. When I "feel" weak, I trust the promise that says, "In my weakness, HE is my strength!" When call reluctance or fear tries to contain me, I take another step of faith and when I do, fear flees. Remember, we're talking about the God factor in the "calling" of sales.

When we are processing Christianity through the wrong filter, we tend to relate to God based on feelings. In other words, if I feel like it's so, it must be. The problem is, relying on something as fickle as feelings will leave us unstable and powerless.

The promise that you can do all things through Christ is not tagged with, "If you feel like it or if you can figure it out."

It is a simple promise that faith lays hold of.

When you feel like God is near, it does not mean He is any nearer to you. He said, "I'll never leave you or forsake you." (Heb 13:5) Again, God doesn't tag that promise with "If you feel like it." In fact, we can't even relate to the word "never" from a natural point of view. Never is a God word and a promise that only He can keep. It means certainly not, not at all, by no means-will He ever leave us! He is an ever present help (Ps 46:1)!

At the same time, our senses have not been suspended the moment we became born-again. On the contrary, they've been enhanced. Jesus said to a whole lot of people with ears, "He that has ears to hear, let him hear!"(Mat 11:15) To others He said, "You have eyes but you fail to see." He wasn't talking naturally. The fact is, believers can see beyond what can be seen. We have "extra-sensory" perception. We can see beyond problems and see His promises. We do not have to rely on what things feels like. We are not to be moved by what we see naturally, but by what we see by faith (2Cor 5:7).

"While we do not look at the things which are seen, but at the things which are not seen. For the things which are seen are temporary, but the things which are not seen are eternal." (2Cor 4:18)

People say, at times, sales is a lonely job. Not when you KNOW, HE is with you! We can go beyond the fickleness of natural feelings or reasonings to an extra-sensory perception of knowing!

This knowledge is true power and the supernatural track we are to run on.

We develop and grow in this as we take God at His Word because what He says, is FACT.. Then, by faith, we respond, whether we feel like it or not. We begin to function from a "knowing" that supersedes feelings and accesses the supernatural.

Paul said, "In my weakness, I am strong." (2Cor 12:10) Obviously, he wasn't checking in with his feelings. He was checking in with the FACTS (i.e. What has God said in His Word!)

This knowledge will cause you to break through your limits and lay hold of His limitlessness. If you are strong by faith even when you feel weak, you won't allow feelings to derail you in the field or in life for that matter. I can't tell you how many times this powerful truth has enabled me to take one more step of faith that caused a turn-around in my day.

There is a superior realm of reality beyond this physical world that we can only access by faith. If we don't renew our minds with the Word of God, we become contained by our feelings or what's humanly reasonable settling for the superficial and becoming out of touch with the supernatural.

When this happens, we become limited by our best or even others' best.

But, when we renew our minds and get a vision for the greater One in us, we are out of the box! This is not just about information, it's about revelation. Without revelation, we'll come face to face with what WE can do about our careers or life, which, in terms of purpose, passion and real power, ain't much.

Our limits are not limits to God. As we trust Him, we break through into a new horizon of possibilities. This is not psychological or even positive thinking. This is beyond us and from God.

"Trust in the LORD with all your heart, and lean not on your own understanding;" (Prov 3:5) The key here is to trust Him, not your feelings or what is humanly reasonable.

"In all your ways acknowledge Him,

And He shall direct your paths." (Prov 3:6)

Know Him, know how! No Him, No way!

I must go into my day knowing not only that He is with me and for me, but, according to the Word of God, He is in me. "Greater is He that is in me than He that is in this world!" (1Jn 4:4). We have a resource bigger than what we can do apart from Him. Don't look at what others in your industry are doing, even the best. We're talking about God's SUPER on your natural. Get a vision for this and set new levels of performance by God's grace. Remember, when you do this, glorify God!

Use this as a platform to point others to Christ! Know Him and make Him known.

We walk by faith, not by sight. When we take by faith what God says in His Word as fact, we will not be moved by feelings; we will be moved by knowing.

The Bible talks about the fact that we are in Christ and Christ is in us. Understanding these truths will help you get over yourself and enable you to wear Jesus in your world. It is two sides of the same coin.

In Ian Thomas book The Saving Life of Christ, he put it this way:

"To be in Christ, makes you fit for heaven; but for Christ to be in you, that makes you fit for earth! To be in Christ changes your destination. To know Christ in you, that changes your destiny! The one makes heaven your home; the other makes this world His workshop!"

Chapter 9 What Are Your Thinkin'?

The quality of life we live and our ability to live it has a lot to do with winning the battle in our thinking. Yet, at the same time, the things of God do not originate in our head. It isn't about a positive mental attitude, though embracing these truths is positive and powerful. As was mentioned before, none of us can rise above the way we think about ourselves (Prov 23:7). The moment we accept Christ we are a new creation. Our heart knows but our heads are a work-in-progress. That's why, even though God recreates our spirits in His likeness, we need to renew our thinking. There is nothing passive about this process. We are to cast down thoughts that are inconsistent with the knowledge of God and bring them captive to Christ (2Cor 10:5). The things of God do not exist in a vacuum, so He gives us His thoughts, found in His Word, to replace renegade thoughts we have by living in this world. We are not called to do only what WE can do about any aspect of our lives apart from Him, but what HE can do through us (1The 5:24). Even Einstein, who never professed to have an understanding of the born-again experience, knew there had to be something more. He recognized that the problems of life could not be remedied on the same level that they were created.

God gives us His Word, which are His thoughts and reality in seed form. He begins with the end in mind (i.e. who we really are in Christ). Jesus taught in Mark 4 how the kingdom of God works: it's like a farmer sowing seeds into the ground. He was referring to taking God's Word—His reality in seed form—and sowing it into our hearts until it begins to take root, grows up, and becomes our predominant thoughts. This is a process and no one is an exception to this process.

The Bible is the ultimate truth, the bottom line, the way it really is.

When we renew our minds with the Word and receive it as what it is—final authority and ultimate reality—then we will experience the power of it. Paul said: I am not ashamed of the Gospel of Christ for it is the power of God to those who believe (Rom 1:16). The Gospel is of Christ, the person, not just about principles. In relating to the Word of God through the the filter of who we are in Him, we experience the power of the Gospel. In fact, we are to trust God through a new paradigm; who we are in Christ (2Cor 3:4). Then, believing right, we are empowered to act right. All the promises of God are in Him, yes and amen (i.e. so be it) (2Cor 1:20). Without faith centered on the person of Christ, the promises are a gift unwrapped, and a religious exercise without power. I am convinced that what God so wants to readily give, we make hard to receive.

I remember the story of Houdini. Born in the late 1800s, he became a magician and escape artist. He challenged officials in cities across the country by telling them that even if they put him in a strait jacket and locked him in their most secure jail, he'd be out in a few hours. Several took him up on the challenge and, true to his word, he would be out in a few hours. One city however, had a simple but ingenious plan to outsmart Houdini.

When the day arrived, as thousands watched, he was strapped into the strait jacket and marched into the local prison. As was usually the case, he was out of the straight jacket in a few minutes. However, there was a problem with the prison's iron door- he couldn't pick the lock. Minutes seemed like hours. Just before time ran out, exhausted, he fell against the door and it opened.

You see, the door was never locked, but in his mind he was in a locked-up fortress. What God has already given us in Christ is unlocked and shows up when we receive and act upon it. If we try to earn, measure up or deserve what God has given us in Christ, we are going down the road most traveled, however, it is the wrong road. We're left exhausted. Here is the massive Good News (which is what the word "Gospel" means, we do not have to earn it or measure up to deserve it. If we simply take it by faith and act like it's so, it's then we will see the reality. We begin to lay hold of an ability and wisdom that doesn't originate with us. It is what God deposits in every believer the moment he or she accepts Christ.

The Bible says, "Counsel is in the heart of man as deep waters. But, a man of understanding will draw it out." (Prov 20:5) Can we expect to draw upon God's know-how? Yes, and it gets even better. God will give us wisdom if we simply ask in faith and He won't hold our faults out when He does. There are no "I told you so" remarks from God!

Chapter 10

Redeemed from the Grind

The Bible tells us what will change the drudgery of work to joy on the job. We truly are to be redeemed from the grind.

The grind is carrying a burden we weren't supposed to carry. When life becomes about what WE can do about it without learning how to draw from God's strength, wisdom, and ability, our journey becomes a burden.

Since the fall of man, the curse made life a grind and work a toil, even though it began as a gift. What was supposed to be fulfilling became frustrating. The curse has made what came easy to man, hard and the result was fear, worry, anxiety.

According to statistics over 75% of people are not enjoying what they do for a living and are in search for the next opportunity. Maybe you know what I'm talking about. The problem is, wherever you go, you take yourself with you. In order to take your job and love it, you must win it from the inside out.

At the same time, this is not a self- improvement plan. It starts with a new creation.

Our identity is the law of the lid. In other words, it determines the ceiling of our success, or lack thereof.

It represents our boundaries and limits and in a very real sense, the wall of containment we hit. If we make it our purpose to discover our identity in Christ, we will experience breakthrough from containment and joy on the job.

I remember the story about a bear that was in a low-budget circus. He was being held in a small cage and he would walk the distance of that cage back and forth. People would watch him and at times, some would cruelly flick a lighted cigarette butt in his way or even shards of glass. He would walk on it, fall to the ground, pat his feet, and get up and walk again.

One day, some people saw the plight of the bear and wanted to do something about it. The thought was to get this bear out of the cage and put him into a wildlife preserve with acres and acres of land available for him to roam. He'd have the freedom to go wherever he wanted, no longer contained or, for that matter, abused.

The people fought the owner with a lawsuit to release the bear. Finally, the day came for his liberty. By this time, it had become an event. A crowd of people watched as they opened the cage and let the bear out. Although he had acres to roam, they discovered that he remained true to form and walked the same distance as his cage, back and forth, as though he was still contained. You see, containment was in his mind. Just like this bear, many have been contained by the lies of the enemy.

If we resort to self-help to fix the problem, we wind up building a bigger cage. God didn't create us to draw from that well. It's only in Christ that we are free and have access to an ability beyond our own. It's only as we identify with Him that we discover a new level of know-how, a new level of living and a new freedom from the grind. Jesus said to come to Him, all who are heavy-laden; in other words, those burdened by the grind.

He promises us "rest", which does not mean inactivity; it is empowered activity. This is huge when it comes to what we do during the day because when we work empowered, we not only get better results, but our day becomes less of a drain and more of a joy.

Until we figure out where to look and who we're looking at, we'll be contained.

All failure is broken focus.

When, as a Christian, we lose sight of Christ, we fail, and since life is a marathon and not a sprint, it's only in Christ that we find the standing, staying and sticking power. Isaiah 40:31, in the actual Hebrew, puts it this way: they that expect the Lord shall exchange strengths; in other words, they will go from their strength (or lack thereof) to His. They shall walk and not faint. They shall run and not be weary.

Have you ever felt like you were not up to the task? I have. I've looked at all I'm supposed to do and wondered how in the world am I going to do this?

Then I come back to Him and discover the desire and the power to "just do it!" If we tend to start and not finish, we have stopped looking to Jesus.

The overcoming principle to every challenge always comes back to the person of Christ. Isaiah 26:3-4 the New Living Translation says, "You will keep in perfect peace all who trust in you, all whose thoughts are fixed on you!"

At times, life can give us an ear full of trouble, but as we focus on Christ, we will receive a mind full of peace.

A peaceful mind generates a power and a presence.

Here's the "rest" of the story: the word "peace" means nothing missing, nothing broken, nothing dysfunctional! Inability, insecurity, inadequacy all dissipate when we begin to trust who God says we are in Christ, rather than who we are apart from Him.

Learning to lean on Him requires a different thought process than leaning on ourselves. It requires an effort, but there's no greater energy drain than trying to live life apart from Him.

Jesus is the way, the truth, the life. Whenever I get frustrated or flustered, it is because in the moment, I have stopped knowing it is about Him.

Jesus must become the hub to the wheel of our lives. Pride or Pity is a misplaced confidence in ourselves and in what we can or cannot do.

Psalm 37: 3, "Trust in the Lord and do..."

Taking time to focus on Christ doesn't stop us from being productive; it is how to be more productive.

A revelation of Christ becomes your forward-moving energy, strengthens your weaknesses, tones down your excesses, and gives you an attitude and an aptitude adjustment.

Fixing your eyes on Jesus is the true remedy to any malady.

Chapter 11

God Begins With the End in Mind

Identifying with Christ and gaining a knowledge of Him in us is the paradigm shift that allows us to access ability beyond our own.

The military, when planning a mission will implement a specific strategy. They will look at what they want as an end result and then work backwards planning the steps necessary to achieve what they call a clear end state. Christ is our clear end state. The power of being "in Him" comes as you begin with the end in mind, (i.e. who you are in Christ) and act like it's so. We will then discover the transformational power of the exchanged life. A new level of know-how comes from knowing Him.

Like any other kind of knowledge, we can always know more about Christ in us-only to an infinitely greater degree. Often times, the obstacle to knowing Him is we cannot see beyond who we used to be. We're limited when our world or the Word of God revolves around our good or bad selves. We can either be impressed with ourselves or depressed about ourselves all the while we are obsessed with ourselves! The Gospel message is for us to get over ourselves and know Him.

Otherwise, we find ourselves trying instead of trusting. You will center your career and I might add, your Christianity on how good you can be.

The reason for limits in our lives is we tend to focus on who we used to be and not who we are in Christ.

2 Corinthians 5:17 (The Message) Now we look inside, and what we see is that anyone united with the Messiah gets a fresh start, is created anew. The old life is gone; a new life burgeons! Look at it! All this comes from God!

The Bible explains that there is a true law of attraction. When we become mature in knowing who we are in Christ, we attract the blessing of God. Galatians 4:1-4 talks about the fact that as long as we are immature, we may be an heir to everything but have no more access than someone who is a hired help in the house. We cannot walk around in fear or self-reliance and expect to experience what God calls the blessed life.

If you were ever unsure about your image, God wants to make clear His thoughts towards you. His promises to you are realities to Him. They are His clear end state concerning YOU!

"God said, "Let us make man in our image, after our likeness: and let them have dominion. So God created man in his *own* image, in the image of God created he him; male and female created he them.

And God blessed them, and God said unto them, Be fruitful, and multiply, and replenish the earth, and subdue it: and have dominion." (Gen 1:26-28)

"For whom He foreknew, He also predestined *to be* conformed to the image of His Son." (Rom 8:29)

God pre-designed us from the start to be fashioned in the same mold and image of His son according to the exact blueprint of His thought. We see the original pattern of our lives in His Son. Christ confirms that we are the invention of God!

"All of us have had that veil removed so that we can be mirrors that brightly reflect the glory of the Lord. And as the Spirit of the Lord works within us, we become more and more like him and reflect his glory even more." (2 Corinthians 3:18)

"Put on the new *man*, which is renewed in knowledge after the image of Him that created him." (Col 3:10)

God's has no hesitation in this. His certainty needs to become our persuasion and then we will see His power. The fact is, how we see ourselves represents the ceiling of our success or lack thereof. It is the wall of containment that we hit and becomes the man made boundaries and borders that limits our impact. It's only as we identify with Him that we begin to break through the containment of stinkin' thinkin! He is actually called, the Lord of the Breakthrough.

You have a different status before God, not based on how good you are but on what He has done. It isn't achieved, it is received. Until we renew our minds, we will live identifying with the old nature and what WE can do versus our new nature and what HE can do through us.

Until you identify with Christ, you will be in touch with the lesser one instead of the greater One.

We don't need another New Year's resolution; we need a New Creation revelation. Learn to let Christ arise in you. The world is looking for the reality of Christ, not the religions of men. God's people need to know He is with them, for them, and in them, so their image of who they were BC (before Christ) will not limit, defeat, or deceive them.

There is no self-image or self-esteem or self-concept that is accurate or empowered which is not centered upon God's clear end state, Christ in us.

Substitutes never satisfy nor empower. This is the mystery and the master key to a new way of living and a new level of SUPERnatural selling.

God wants His people to draw from His strength, with an awareness of Him. He wants us to honor Him in whatever we're called to do. When we achieve an excellence that causes men to ask, "How do you do it?' you can tell them about Him.

We have allowed our limited understanding to limit an infinite God. They that know Him shall be strong and do exploits (Dan 11:32). You begin to affect people at another level; your life begins to be an influence beyond you. Principles in this book are applicable in every area of your life. I have had the pleasure of sharing much of the content in this book nationally with some of the best sales people in the country. I have watched lives impacted on the job and in other areas of my life and ministry. I recently taught some of these concepts on a platform that reached people in 85 countries.

I have seen many lives impacted. I tell you this so you understand that there are things that happen to us and through us when we get our thinking straight. It affects everything we are and everything we do. These concepts influence people regardless of their calling or career. I have two daughters that both impact their world for Christ. One is a successful businesswoman and the other is a Christian recording artist. We can never do without God what He can do through us.

Don't limit yourself to being a self-made man or woman. It is God who has made you. Your new DNA in Christ is SUPERnatural.

Chapter 12

The Wow Factor

The book entitled, *The Present* by Spencer Johnson has some profound truth in it. Yet, as with everything I read, I examine it in the light of God's Word. Anything that has real truth in it and principles that actually work can be traced to the Bible. This book is no exception. *The Present*, is a play on words and it's about living in the moment. The Present is a gift which keeps on giving. Johnson maintains that learning to live in the NOW changes everything. We become more productive, effective, and we discover more joy and satisfaction in this journey we call life.

Life is a gift discovered in the present.

David said, "Teach us to number our days that our hearts may apply wisdom." (Ps 90:12) Think about how we rob our now and how unwise it is to worry. Worry is the past and the future haunting us, all the while the now gets lost. If we don't learn how to stop and enjoy the moment, smell the flowers, dial into the people we are with, we'll never tap into the richness that's all around us.

The fact is, we can wring our hands about the past or worry about the future, but when we do, we lose the gift of the present. The real secret to living can only be found in the moment. Isaiah 43:18-19, NIV translation, says, "Forget the former things; don't dwell on the past. See, I am doing a new thing! **NOW** it springs up; do you not perceive it? I am making a way in the desert and streams in the wasteland."

God didn't promise us a life without challenges. Instead, He shows us how to respond so we can experience true living. The first lesson of experiencing a quality present is to forget the past. We are to learn from, not dwell on, the past. Learning from mistakes and then letting them go is a critical lesson in living a quality now. The second lesson is that we must open our eyes to the new thing God's doing. Whatever the challenge, God can turn it around. This is a faith principle. Faith is how we see, perceive, and overcome. The Bible says we are to live by faith. Here's the rest of the story: Hebrews 11:1 starts by saying, "Now, faith is." Real faith is found now and is how we are to lay hold of the promises of God before we see them and the victory before we experience it. Until we purpose to live by faith, we will live as victims and not victors. Perceptions are inaccurate when the only vantage point is outside-in. When the spring is found in a dry place and the peace is discovered in the midst of a storm, both are an inside-out proposition. Accurate perception is the result of walking by faith, not by natural sight. It's the ultimate attitude and aptitude adjustor!

"Faith comes from hearing, hearing the Word of God."(Rom 10:17) Repetition is intentional here. What we continually hear in the Word causes faith to arise. At the same time, fear comes from hearing, hearing the word of the world. In other words, what we hear repeatedly feeds our faith or our fears. If we're going to be a positive influence, which is what selling the right way is, we are going to have to have the light on in our own hearts! Here's the reality: when things in life and work become an adventure, it isn't because things changed. It's because we did!

By faith we find perspective, focus, ability, and the right attitude.

The now is the *wow* of life. The now is found by faith.

I heard a song by Big Daddy Weave. A portion of the lyrics said:

Up tight, down right, wound up like a spring.

Funny how I worry about what doesn't mean a thing,

But that's when you speak truth to me,

The chorus settles the matter:

I'm in less of a hurry,

I'm less likely to worry,

When in my heart I receive thoughts of my eternal destiny. I've given up frustration,

Trust you without hesitation,

It must be the You in me.

We need to let Christ dwell in our heart by faith and let Him arise. When we do, we'll be alive in the moment and a positive and powerful influence on others.

Chapter 13

Influence and the Lesson of the Iceberg

Everyone influences, so everyone sells. If you are in any kind of a relationship, or you are communicating at all, much of it is about influence. Intentional or not, even if we are just giving our opinion, make no mistake about it: some level of selling is involved. Persuading your kids to do the right thing involves selling. The preacher who preaches the Gospel or the person called to be a leader are only effective to the degree that they influence. The important thing to remember is that God wants us to be an influence, for the right reasons and with the right motives. Before you're off to the races about this and start "trying", I'm going to show you how to do this gracefully by trusting. The Gospel means GOOD NEWS and it is the power of God to those who trust, not to those who try. Early in my career, I would tend to focus on the commission. When my thoughts gravitated towards the dollars, I would get a ping in my heart, a kind of out-of-sync feeling. I soon realized God was wanting me to focus on meeting the need of others as the priority. Initially, I didn't understand how this worked so I wore the correction as guilt.

As I matured, I learned to receive the correction but then also trust that I am who He says I am in Christ. Let me explain. Every time I put cash before the cause and got that ping, I would say to the Lord, *"I see it. I make that correction and now...I leave it with you!"* Then, in faith, I would agree with Him that I am a new creation in Christ and I do what I do for the right reasons. Sometimes it doesn't feel like it, but to grow up, we must go beyond feelings into knowing. As I have gotten a hold of this truth, I can honestly say it has gotten a hold of me. I am not conflicted anymore and people recognize my sincerity in wanting to discover and meet their needs and I am passionate about it. What I have been selling for years affects our freedoms and is very cause oriented.

I was in a sales interview with someone who, after I answered several of his objections, said to me, "I am going to do this because I can see this is about the cause with you and not the cash, is that true?" I answered him by saying, "For the most part! But, if I get that out of order, I don't need anyone to tell me about it, God does!" He appreciated my honesty and bought. I don't approach my Christianity as me being holier-than-thou. I live this life, real before God and people.

I refuse to be pressured to make a sale. I am focused on being a blessing and the sales take care of themselves. This is not a technique. It is a core level conviction.

When you're honest before God, He will teach you how to do sales right so you can spend your day on the give and blessed, which is a whole lot better than being on the take and stressed.

God's way in 'sanctified" and supernatural selling is we are blessed financially when we add value and keep first things first.

God, our Father, is a God of the heart, and so intent is important to Him. Learning to draw from a well of conviction so that your words carry weight and help people come to the right conclusion is a powerful principle not just to be successful in sales, but in life. This well of conviction is bottomless and when we learn to draw from it, our firm conviction can overcome the strongest resistance.

God will empower and enable us if in our heart we purpose to be on the give. The whole sales experience becomes a win-win proposition. God has always wanted to be invited into the process, and doing it His way changes the profession of sales into not just a successful long term career, but a "high" calling.

Think of it this way: the quickest way from point A to point B is a straight line.

For the sake of illustration, the **A**=Activity, quality and quantity activity. (Is there any substitute?) We must do enough and do it correctly to get results on purpose.

B=Business. In other words, results.... If we stay on the straight line, we'll be more productive in less time.

However, the reality is that somewhere along the way we encounter the **C**—you know, the Challenge. The twists and turns, the setbacks, etc. It's the fork in the road that may take many forms, but often times, the root of it is a crisis of conviction.

It begs the question: Do you believe you can do this?

Do you believe what you offer is truly meeting a need?

Note: *If you don't believe in what you're selling, look for something you can believe in.*

God, who is our Father, uses the canvas of creation to teach us important life lessons. Icebergs vary in size, but what we see represents less than 10 percent. It is only the "tip" of the iceberg. Beneath the surface are the qualities of the iceberg that teach us some powerful truths.

Although surrounded by oceans and beat up by waves, icebergs seem to move at their own pace. Some are even large enough to change currents. If the mass beneath the surface loses density, the iceberg becomes unstable, loses forward motion, and eventually will be no more.

What's the lesson to us? We can't have a "Shallow-Hal" approach if we're going to be an influence for good and for God or if we want to have a long lasting career.

If we're going to relentlessly move forward and not quit, we must understand there needs to be more beneath the surface than above.

Most celebrate breadth; we must cultivate depth by fueling our conviction. A faith-infused, belief-filled attitude leads to high level interviews with high level results. There's no bottom to this. It changes the currents of resistance and isn't subject to them. I have trained some top producers who have experienced a crisis of conviction. They hit the proverbial wall where increasing the number of sales interviews did not increase results. You can be professional and lose your passion which leads to a lessoning in persuasion and call reluctance. When we lose heart, we become peddlers.

We must have our heart and head in the game.

If you ask for a certain dollar amount when you think in your heart of hearts what you're offering is worth one tenth that amount, eventually, you will get burned out. The remedy? Make sure what you offer has value by knowing "why" it meets your customer's needs. Know your competitive advantage. Know "why" what you say is resonating with them because you've taken a walk in their shoes. Hyper-focus on what's important to your customer.

When your "why" is big enough, you'll figure out how! Because I consistently follow this pattern, I believe what I offer has so much value I no longer have a crisis of conviction when I ask them to invest, whatever that amount is. This is about having heart in what we do and because God is a God of the heart, this is selling His way.

When our "why" is crystal clear, the current of customers' resistance can be overcome by our fortified belief.

Gross calls are steps of faith. They become quality, quantity, and consistency when we're all-in.

I'll only have the right response in the context of core level conviction, which always stems from right believing.

This belief spills over into our ability to do what we do with excellence and effectiveness which is not about bravado or being all you can be or even self-confidence. Instead, it is confidence in God who says, nothing is impossible to those who believe!

When we face our giants, God is there. Jesus said, in the world we would have challenges. Without trials we're an empty page, a blank notebook, a missing lyric. We are to count it all joy when we encounter various trials (Jas 1:2). Why? It's because trials will work out of us what God's put in us. In Christ, He's given us what it takes to overcome; faith, love, joy, peace, patience, self-control, etc.

If we'll draw from the well of the new creation, we can bring heart. These prevailing forces of our born-again spirit will exert an overcoming influence on the challenges of life.

We can laugh, when we feel like crying.

Be in faith even when we feel fear.

Run, even when it feels like we can't take another step.

We can overcome the pain, push through to breakthrough until we become stronger, more courageous, and more confident.

Pressure can cause us to depend on who we were before we met Christ. Instead, trust Him, take another step. Expect Him, be infused with His strength. Know Him, be empowered to DO life. This is how we engage our heart and draw from the Greater One in us!

Chapter 14
A Revolutionary Way to Sell....

God, our Father, knows sales. Remember, the original definition of sales is, "to give." This is a Biblical concept that God endorses wholeheartedly. He so loved that He gave His Son.

It goes without saying, what we sell, in terms of importance, is not on the same level. Yet, we have to learn to glean principles from the Word because they're applicable in life. Our purpose is to be a blessing. When we do sales His way, He gives you the ability to do more in less time with less stress.

In the context of "giving," you'll discover you're more professional, purposeful, and productive, all the while accessing His power and presence.

You can't over-spiritualize stories in the Bible if you want to learn from them. Some criticize by saying, "You're so heavenly minded, you're no earthly good." The exact opposite is actually the truth. There are people who are spooky-spiritual and they truly are no earthly good. Heaven is more real than earth. In John 4, I was reading about the woman at the well, and the Lord gave me an interesting perspective.

This woman was a real person who had experienced bad relationships. She had been hurt and taken advantage of. Her trust had been violated.

She finds Jesus as her savior which is the best news of all, but I want you to see something we can glean from this in our everyday experience. Her resistance was distrust which can easily spill over into all kinds of human interaction when trust has been violated. Many people we talk with have their walls up and are questioning whether what you're offering is of value, importance or for that matter, urgent. Throw into the mix that they're questioning your motives. Jesus knew what He was offering even while this woman questioned his motives. He stood His ground with statements born out of conviction. Something He was fully persuaded about. Do you know why what you offer is important? Are you convinced it would be beneficial? A blessing? The same principle applies. When you know your offer meets your potential customer's need, you can stand your ground and speak with a conviction that God will give you. When love is involved, so is God!

The woman at the well insulted Jesus, questioned His motives, and misunderstood Him. If you're in sales, you've experienced all of the above.

But Jesus is the master influencer for the right reasons. He knew He was the most important person she would see that day and ever.

Do you begin your day knowing you have something beneficial to offer?

Pray for those you expect to see and God will help you know the right thing to say.

Personally I pray that not only will I bless people by meeting their earthly needs, but also, when I have the opportunity, I share how Christ will meet their ultimate need.

This journey we call life becomes an adventure when it is about knowing Him and making Him known!

Chapter 15

Be Still

"Be still, and know that I am God!"

(Ps 46:10)

A blind man was begging on a busy street corner for money. On a cardboard sign, next to an empty tin cup, he had written: *Blind - Please help*. No one stopped.

A young man who was a copy writer for an advertising company walked past and saw the blind man with his sign and empty cup. He noticed people rushing by completely unmoved, let alone stopping to give money.

The young man took a thick marker from his pocket, turned the cardboard sheet over, and re-wrote the sign, then went on his way.

Immediately, people began putting money into the tin cup.

After a while, when the cup was overflowing, the blind man asked a stranger to tell him what the sign said.

"It says: It's a beautiful day. You can see it. I cannot.'"

The still is a place where we see, not just with natural eyes, but God's eyes.

I used to think I was too busy to be still. I soon discovered I was too busy *NOT* to be still. This is counterintuitive to a generation that is amped up and in a hurry. I can be in the day He has made or settle for the day I have made. It all depends on how I start my day; from the still or on the run.

There is an exchange made when I wait on Him. Taking a pause on purpose, we can learn to access an ability beyond our own.

Christ becomes our source and sufficiency which, when it's all said and done, is supernatural. It is revelation and then demonstration.

Jesus not only showed the way, but He paved the way for us to have quality time with our Father by giving us His righteousness (right standing) (2Cor 5:21) and letting us know, we are loved the same way He is loved (Jn17:23). This means, I don't have to hesitate and I can come to Him without reservation. This is not because of how good I am, but how great He is. This becomes the basis for not just coming to God, but connecting with Him when I do. The spirit of man is the candle of the Lord (Pro 20:27).The still is where the things of God dawn on me. New creation realities of who I am in Christ are discovered, amplified and imparted there. That includes my identity-who I am, my inheritance-what I have, my influence/impact-what I can do!

God will put His SUPER on our natural in the still.

David was a man after God's heart. His life was centered on connecting with God in the still. He wasn't satisfied to be at a distance.

He refused religious concepts about a God who is half-mad at us. I remember a preacher once saying "If a donkey goes to the watering trough every day and someone hits him on the head with a two-by-four and yells, "God", that donkey doesn't have to be real smart to figure out he doesn't want to have anything to do with God! Here's the point: the two-by-four isn't God. The basis for connecting with Him in the still is that we know His heart. When we do, we run to Him instead of from Him. Until then, we've got the cart before the horse (or the donkey and that means we aren't going anywhere fast or growing anytime soon.

What did David know that revolutionized his life?

In Psalm 139, he realized that God knew his thoughts before he thought them and his words before he spoke them. It dawned on Him that God understood and knew him best, loved him most, and that His opinion was the only one that mattered. He realized that God had been to every event and was with him every moment of every day. You become aware of Him in your day when you've taken time to be with Him in the still.

He is so involved in every detail of our lives that He had the first baby book. I'm not making this up. Psalm 139, Verse 16 of the New Living Translation puts it this way:

You saw me before I was born. Every day of my life was recorded in your book. Every moment was laid out before a single day had passed."

Do you realize that God hasn't stopped writing your story?

We are all driven in some ways to perform. Sales, is by no means an exception. Trusting God, you access new levels of productivity. But, in the still, it comes to us on His terms. He doesn't start with how good we are. David understood, "If I am on the highest high or lowest low, at a distance or in the darkness, He is there; it's all light and love from Him towards me. How good I get it, or how much I measured up to the standard, whether I prayed enough or read my Bible enough, etc.; all of these things are good, but they have a starting point. A place where faith possesses grace.

These are the fruit of correctly believing and are the cause and effect of Christianity.

How I let go and let God.

As I choose to believe, I have the light and love that floods me and casts out all fear.

The fear of a misstep, the fear of separation, the sense that God is at a distance all are swallowed up in this Psalm which is a picture of the heart of our Father.

He is in pursuit of us on our worst or best day. He is always the same—love personified, love in essence and in action.

He is not a fair-weather friend or Father; He is an ever-present help. He is the one in pursuit of you all the days of your life (Ps 23:6). When you stop running at life like a bull in a china closet and live life from the still, you will rise above the storms, where the Son has always been shining. This is a transformational message that impacts our productivity on the job and in life period. Knowing the heart of God, should always cause you to run TO Him and not from Him. He is for us, with us, and in New Testament terms, in us. Even with all of his flaws, David knew God was thinking about him 24/7 and His thoughts were precious (Ps 139:17). He knew he was greatly loved and valued and that God saw beyond his obvious failings. In New Testament terms, God sees our spirit created in the image of Christ. He places us in Him, gives us His right standing, calls us sons, and then gives us an ability beyond our own.

Those that know Him will be strong and do exploits (Dan 11:32)! Sounds like the language of a SUPERnatural salesperson, doesn't it? When we are in the habit of starting our day from the still, we learn to rely on Him.

This is how we become a light on a hill that points others to Him. You will make history as you tell His story through your profession.

It is our Father's great joy when we connect with Him at the heart-level and allow His Spirit to reveal Christ in us. We are on a journey to know Him as our source, sufficiency, our security and our identity where He becomes what He is, The Way, the Truth, and the Life;

The Way (we do what we do),

The Truth (that we can do all things through Christ), and

The Life (in what we do).

The next chapter of our lives will be written in the still. Make it a God one!

Chapter 16

The "Rest" of the Story is Discovered in the Still

Learning how to come at life from the still is the secret to living the abundant life Jesus promised. (Jn 10:10)

Redeeming the time (Eph 5:16) or making the most of every opportunity is only accomplished as we recalibrate our hearts to be in tune with God's heart. He wants to lead us, so rather than running at life with our eyes closed, we can have our steps ordered.

It is as we purpose to pause and seek Him first that He equips us for whatever the day may bring. If we allow the clamor of a "to do" list undone to rob us from being still, we will carry the weight of our world and, have you discovered, all that does is wear you out?

In the still there is a rest, refreshing and revitalization. Biblical rest doesn't mean we don't do anything. It means doing what we do, empowered.

In other words, you can rest while working, you can rest while living and you can stop carrying the burdens of life. Jesus said to those who had not learned the lesson from the still, "Come to Me all who are burdened, weighed down; I will give you rest." (Mat 11:28). Coming to Christ is a lesson from the still that allows us to let go and let God.

You can stop the madness of saying to Him, "*I'll take it from here.*"

As salespeople, we want to be go-getters, yet if we get this, we will get it, whatever it is!

There is a refreshing in the presence of the Lord. Most of us are in the smog of a flurry of activity. We haven't stopped to take a breath. The still reinvigorates us from the stale. Our careers can become stimulating when our perspective is from the still, but keep running at life on fumes and what we do will become boring, lifeless, purposeless, passionless, powerless—what of any of that do you want? We're trying to figure out life. God wants us to faith it out. Romans 10:17 says, "Faith comes by hearing and hearing by the Word of God."

So before you start your day, spend time in the Word. God can communicate anyway He wants but it is rarely audible and He will never say something inconsistent with His Word.

To experience that heart level connection with Him by, you first of all must know, His greatest desire is to spend time with you. First Corinthians 1:9 says, "He is faithful who has called us to fellowship (i.e. heart to heart intimacy)."

The word for called in this verse means as if He called you personally by name.

If we don't take what He says to us personally, it will never be powerful! In His faithfulness and His desire to spend quality time with us, He bankrupted heaven, and sent His Son to die for us so we can come to Him without reservation. From God's point of view, we're clothed in Christ (Gal 3:27). If we understand that Jesus became our every failure and gave us His right standing (2Cor 5:21) and that we are loved by the Father the way He is (Jn 17:23), we will then come to Him not timidly, but with boldness, not because of what we've done, but because of what He's done! This is the basis for our quiet time being quality time where we connect with Him and we discover purpose, passion and power. Our fire, freedom and functionality come to us from this place of heart to heart communion.

As I begin my time with Him, I pause for direction. The more you practice this, the more leading you will have. If I don't sense a specific direction, I may read a Psalm, or a Proverb for the day (there are 31 chapters, 1 for each day of the month) or something else from Scripture. I spend a lot of time in the New Testament Epistles (i.e. Romans to Jude) because the Word of God is progressive in revelation and the Epistles are where I discover who I am in Christ which makes everything else I read in the Bible make sense. He is the Word made flesh. He is the context, the crescendo, and the cause to empowered Christianity.

The point is, I am not in a hurry because I am expecting something from the Word to stand out to me, like an "aha" moment or the light just went on. This is the way God communicates His thoughts. "The spirit of man is the lamp of the Lord" (Prov 20:27) In other words, where the things of God dawn on us). The more you purpose to seek God first, the more you will learn to pick up on His thoughts, not just in your quiet time, but throughout the day. The Bible contains God's thoughts and is the foundation for how He speaks. Like the instructions of a loving parent, here is the dynamic of what happens when you keep His thoughts from His Word in your heart, "When you walk, they will guide you; when you sleep, they will watch over you; when you awake, they will speak to you." (Pro 6:22) It goes on to say His Word is a lamp to your feet and a light to your path. As you quiet yourself and turn your heart towards Him, you will begin to get impressions and streams of thought with a depth of wisdom and knowledge that you could never have accessed on the run. As a coach, mentor and sales trainer, these times have led to creative ideas that have profoundly impacted not only me personally, but top producers I have been blessed to train. This is a lifestyle that affects not only how productive you are, but how you parent, or how you do anything of consequence for that matter. It is truly, a game changer.

When I'm intentional about being still, I can draw from a well that is limitless and learn to trust that God will put His super on my natural!

Chapter 17

Purpose-Driven/The Heart of the Matter

Disney produces some amazing films. Recently, I was watching a documentary with my grandchildren that was a unique up-close-and-personal glimpse of chimpanzees in a rarely seen habitat, the Tai Forest in the Ivory Coast of Africa.

The storyline involves two groups of rival chimps. The star is a three-year-old monkey that they named Oscar. After a brief but fierce fight, his mother dies and the smaller troop of chimps are exiled from their territory. Now orphaned, Oscar is left to fend for himself. The other females rejected him but something happened that amazed everyone involved with this film. Totally out of character, the gray-haired alpha male, that they had named Fred, took Oscar under his wing.

The documentary chronicles their relationship. These weren't actors following a script nor was it an animation; it was a real-life drama unfolding in front of their cameras.

This was an amazing turn of events because orphaned young'uns like Oscar are pretty much doomed and alpha males in the wild are not likely to be nurturing. When another battle ensues between these two groups over food and territory, instead of running like he had previously, Fred ran at the leader of the rival band of chimps. The gory details of what actually happened can be researched, but, because of the age of the audience the filmmakers wanted to reach, they kept the violent scenes to a minimum. A fierce fight erupted between Fred, the older alpha male, and the younger powerful alpha leader of the larger group. Fred, who looked like he was possessed with a new sense of vitality and total lack of concern for himself, soundly defeated his rival, who limped away from the battle.

My grandchildren had long since gone off to play with their toys but I was mesmerized by what I just saw. The Bible talks about the fact that nature will teach us a lesson.

The Lord used this to illustrate a powerful truth about the purpose-driven life. You see, the stakes were changed. Fred's cause changed from the hunt for bananas to the greater purpose of protecting the life of his newly adopted son. Fred, if you will, had a transcendent purpose that kept him from running, even though he was outnumbered and was seemingly no match for his adversary.

A deeper sense of purpose beyond one's self gives a dimension of passion, power, and persistence that nothing else can. It is not uncommon for people to put their lives at risk in the service of a cause they deeply believe in.

For example, money is a motivator, but it has limits.

Think about this: while money serves as a primary source of motivation and preoccupation for many, researchers have found almost no correlation between income levels and happiness. Between 1957 and 1990, per-person income in the United States doubled. Not only did people's reported levels of happiness fail to increase at all during that period, but rates of depression grew nearly tenfold. The incidence of divorce, suicide, and alcoholism and drug abuse dramatically increased. Money is important, but it should be the result of our pursuit of purpose, not become the purpose we pursue, or we will run from the challenge.

Jim Collins makes the compelling case in his book "Built to Last" that purpose-driven companies have far superior results over the long haul. Strongly held value-driven purpose is the "all-in" principle in every arena of our lives. We bring passion, commitment, and perseverance to whatever we do in direct proportion to the clear-cut purpose we have.

Have you noticed that sales isn't always easy?

There are times when we must endure difficult and stressful work environments. When we are intentional about living in concert with a clear purpose, we can continue to make choices about how to behave from a position of courage, confidence, and conviction, rather than cave when things become challenging. When we discover purpose in what we do, we'll find the heart of the matter. If a monkey can do it....just sayin'!

Chapter 18

The Golden Rule

The book by Bob Burg and John David Mann entitled, *Go -Givers Sell More* is powerful when we consider it in light of the Bible.

Have you considered that what's most important in the interview process is not just about the product?

We do need to be prepared beforehand, know our competitive advantage, etc. yet in order for there to be a connection, the focal point needs to be about creating value. This happens in the moment and on a personal level.

This changes the interview process from just quantity to quality! Both are needed but, I've seen people passionate about the product, but there was a disconnect in the presentation. Don't get me wrong, it's better that we believe in what we're offering than not. But, what I'm talking about is reps who are zealous about what THEY think is most important but the potential customer never hears a word because they're stuck at their interest or angst. We need to be prepared for anything, but know not to say everything! High Level or High Trust selling is not about us.

It is about the other person. We relate to the customer from his point of view or what we have to say will fall on deaf ears! This is a two-way street. They don't hear us because we haven't heard them! This is heart to heart communication that we must be intentional about.

This would fall under the heading of nuances or the small things that make a huge difference. The dollars truly are in the details.

The essence of the Golden Rule is the more you give, the more you receive. Mathew 6:33, says, "Seek first the kingdom of God and his righteousness, His way of being and doing right, and all these things will be added to you." This flies in the face of a world wired to get all they can and then sit on the can! Putting the love factor of giving into the interview process changes everything. The stress is less because our purpose is right! The way the kingdom of God works is giving never depletes. It multiplies.

"Whoever sows sparingly will reap sparingly, and whoever sows bountifully will reap bountifully." (2Cor 9:6). In other words, the more we give, the more we receive!

"The task here is not to create value in order to create a sale or "in order to" do anything. It's to create value period!" (*Go Givers Sell More*) Obviously, to be successful, sales need to happen.

Here is the paradox, in order for a predictable outcome to occur, we must set aside the idea of the sale and make our job providing value.

If we do that well, success will follow.

"Money is the echo of value! It is the thunder of values lightning! Create value and money follows! It has to!"

The question of does what we do make money is not a bad question to ask in any endeavor we pursue. It's a great question. It's just a bad first question! The first question that must be asked is: Does it serve? Does it add value, meet a need?" (*Go Givers Sell More*)

If you know in your heart it does, then you won't have to ask, will it make money. It will not only make you an income, it will become a satisfying long term career. Putting money first doesn't work. The truth is, denying money or pretending it doesn't matter won't work either. This is just about proper perspective and purpose in the sales process. You may be acting for another's benefit or your own, but you can't do both at once.

This cognitive dissonance causes a lack of conviction and that is never good when it comes to communication that influences for the right reasons! When we purpose to give, we have less of an internal conflict!

If you get a ping in your heart that you are out of bounds, fess up and begin trusting that since you've accepted Christ, you're wired to give.

Here's another powerful statement from the book, "Go-Givers Sell More", which is consistent with a Biblical approach to what I would describe as sanctified and SUPERnatural selling, "The true giver knows that giving is a tide that raises all ships and that it allows you to be a person of value to others while doing very well for yourself!" I can only say one thing to that....Amen!

Chapter 19

Stewards of Professionalism and Passion

Our words carry conviction when we believe what we are saying. In order to reach people at their core, we must have words that come from an aligning of our head and our heart; not just professional, but passionate—and, may I say, persuaded?

I've discovered some critical components in what might best be called faith-based selling. Galatians 5:6 says, Faith works by love. Love is the foundational motive for faith and faith will not work without it! Love requires that I am on the give. I consistently take the time to take a walk in my potential customer's shoes, not just a little, but the extra mile.

I believe what I am saying and I know why I am saying it because I know who the customer is. When I meet them, I'm not just in their office; I'm in their world. There are only so many things that can come up in a sales interview, so if I want to be professional, passionate, and persuasive because I am personally persuaded, I must be prepared.

Being fully persuaded myself has taken those I have trained and myself to another level of effectiveness and empowerment. I learned a lesson from Abraham's life. He was having a difficult time believing God. He wanted children, but he was well past the age and his wife Sarah, had been barren all her life. God made him a promise but Abraham just could not see it. Maybe you've been there. Abraham's situation became even more hopeless with every passing year. When he was 100 years old and his wife Sarah was 90 years old, God did something that caused faith to arise in Abraham's heart. Nothing in the Word of God is accidental or incidental and it isn't meant for the sake of Biblical characters alone. It was meant to teach us principles we can apply. The lesson? Find someone who has results, do what they do and you will have predictable outcomes. In Genesis 15, God told Abraham to look up at the stars and then said, "So shall your seed be." In other words, God helped Abraham see the promise and the positive outcome. Faith arose in his heart and Romans 4:18-21 gives us the details of what happened next. It says he did not stagger at the promises of God or the hopelessness of the situation, instead he grew strong in faith. Verse 21 sums it up by saying that he became fully persuaded that what God promised he was able to perform. When we are in faith, we gain posture and presence because we are fully persuaded.

2Corinthians 4:16 illustrates this process. We don't lose heart because our inward man is renewed day by day. In our terms, we grow stronger in faith and we have more conviction daily.

Verse 17 says our light affliction is for a moment, but it puts something to work for us that carries a far exceeding and eternal weight. Affliction here can represent things that don't go well, or brings discouragement, etc., but the weight of belief will outweigh any hopelessness or discouragement we may face.

Verse18 is the master key. While we look not at the things which are seen, but at the things that are not; In other words, faith sees the promise, and the positive outcome which results in overcoming the challenge. Does it work? Does it make a difference Monday morning? Not too long ago, I met with a customer. The year before, he had invested a substantial amount of $5000. Prayerfully, I went through the process of thinking about what his needs might be. I remembered what mattered to him. I thought about our competitive advantage. I asked the Lord to help me see the positive outcome. In my heart, I heard and saw the customer say, *Dan, thank you for what you said because I hadn't seen that before.*

In prayer, I saw him say yes to investing $10k. I wasn't even thinking about asking him for that amount, but that figure came to my heart so I asked in faith. I didn't do this to manipulate the outcome. Remember, faith works by love. I also, didn't do it to manipulate God. I asked Him to help me see so I could be what I needed to be: professional, passionate, and fully persuaded. We owe it to the people we serve to be all-in. If what we do meets their need, it doesn't do our customer any good if we play small ball.

By the way, if he didn't buy, part of Biblical faith is to roll the care of the results to the Lord and be unattached to the outcome. What happened in the interview? After twenty minutes, he said to me, "Dan, I hadn't seen it that way before. I'll invest $10k." When I got back into the car, I could only do one thing: Thank God for His faithfulness, His wisdom, and His Word!

Chapter 20

L.I.S.T.E.N.

I was landing in Kansas City when the flight attendant came on the intercom and said, "You could have chosen another airline, but we sincerely thank you for flying Southwest. Keep in mind, as you open the bins, do so with caution because the baggage may have shifted and could fall out on you or others and we don't want to have to do the paperwork!"

Everyone laughed and it was meant to be funny, but I sat there thinking, "Wow, how often do we project insincerity, lack of conviction or cluelessness in our attempt to communicate our message. Like one person said "The single biggest problem with communication is the illusion that it has taken place."

Communication that causes us to connect and build trust is made with the heart, not just the tongue.

When the trust level is high, communication becomes easy and effective. To remember, think about the word LISTEN as an acronym.

L.I.S.T.E.N

The "L" stands for Listen. Communication may be a two-way street but listening is the highway.

James 1:19 NIV translation says, "Everyone should make note of this. Be quick to hear, slow to speak." Nothing is more disconnecting than getting this out of order.

"I" stands for intentional and intently. Intentional because always being "intentional" about listening should become our purpose.

Intently because we have given time to not just what we say from a script, but what we say because we know who the customer is and "why" we say the words.

Here's a divine paradox. Prov. 17:27 say, "Whoever restrains his words has knowledge."

In our quick-to-speak society, the Bible says, and I am paraphrasing, a fool gushes before he hears!

We've got a lot to say, but what needs to be said is what is important to the customer.

Prov. 17:27 goes on to say that he who has a calm spirit is a man of understanding. When we intentionally spend time thinking about who the customer is, what their needs are, and how our product/service meets those needs, we will then understand how to help them make a decision for their sake. We won't react. We'll calmly respond. We won't fear what someone says. We'll welcome it!

"S" is for sincerity: If we're sincere, it makes up for a lot of what we lack in presentation skills.

If we are not, no matter how good our presentation, it will always be lacking. We must learn the mechanics for sure, but for it to be effective, it must be sincere

"T" stands for Tune in. God will give us discernment so we can read the customer and know how to relate and resonate with them. What we say won't be "Just Words!" The walls of distrust will come down and we will be an encouragement for them to take action for the right reasons. Proverbs 15:23 MSG translation says: Everyone enjoys a fitting reply; it is wonderful to say the right thing at the right time!

The letter "E" stands for empathy. It doesn't mean I pull up a stool and cry alongside of people. It really means, we are not ignoring their concerns, but like as a light set on a hill, we bring "the rest of the story" so we can encourage them to do what's in their best interest.

"N" stands for NEVER. NEVER, even though you have a lot to say, say it all, never assume that communication works without working at it. Never forget to study your "why" this is important to the customer. It is the weight of your words. Never lose sight of the purpose to listen, discover needs and know why what you offer will meet those needs. When you do, you will have greater results with less stress.

Chapter 21

Communication: Are You Building Walls or Bridges?

Are we building walls or bridges? The weight of words that have conviction and a well thought out "why" carry influence that is hard to resist.

Proverbs 25:15 in the Message Bible says, Patient persistence pierces through indifference, and gentle speech breaks down ridged defenses.

Let's face it, the people we talk with are bombarded with someone with something to sell. Add to that the clutter that comes with every other form of media from billboards to Facebook and there is a whole lot of talking going on. What makes what we say get past the clutter and count? A lot of people talk, but few connect. The reality is talk is cheap, but connecting is priceless. In the sales process, connecting is the ability to identify with people in a way that increases your influence with them because you purpose to discover and meet their needs.

When we, from our heart, carry the higher ideal of a well-thought out, reinforced why, the strongest resistance is overcome.

Our "Why" is what gives the sales process, purpose and meaning. Whenever we raise the bar on why we find the words when we don't have the words, and we have influence because people sense the heart in what we're saying.

It is never a good idea to not have the words on time; in fact, Proverbs 15:28 says that the righteous study how to answer. At the same time, if you only have polish without passion it's like a clanging cymbal. Technique cannot replace sincerity any more than ceremony can substitute for substance.

Proverbs 15:23, in the common English Bible, says "To give an appropriate answer is a joy. How good is a word at the right time?"

I saw a Sprint commercial that illustrates this point. A professional football player was on a gurney with his knee wrapped and his doctor at his bedside.

The football player said, "Doc, I got your text that said I'm out for the season?" The doctor replied, "Oh, don't worry. I have Sprint and I've got unlimited text." The player said, "What? I don't care about that. What's with my knee?" the response was, "Oh, that. You took a vicious hit; you're out for the season. Do you want to see it?" The athlete is now all-in with his body language and says, "No, I don't want to see it!" And the doctor, who is clueless, says, "Oh, don't worry, I have unlimited video!"

If we don't hear the customer in the context of his why, we won't give an appropriate answer and, I might add, we'll be fortifying a wall instead of building a bridge.

This is not an issue. It is *the* issue!

I train reps to not only anticipate what's important to the customer, but also to see them happily involved. The weight of a thought has our minds firing on about two-thousand neutrons, according to some researchers. Thought carried with an image fires up about 40 billion neutrons. The "One Minute Sales Person" talks about the fact that top producers do a one-minute commercial of the interview in their mind. They imagine the need, their answer, and the happy ending. As I prayed about that statement, I was impressed to keep a journal and write down not just the important words that were exchanged, but the emotion of what was said. Also, I think about and write down how the customer went from someone whose walls were up to someone I connected with on a meaningful level. This is textbook selling for doing business by "THE BOOK" and how you develop high level trust which leads to high level results with a whole lot less stress!

Chapter 22

The Key to Influence: Selling at the Speed of Trust

The God who is both infinite and personal not only exists, but He is a communicator. Because we've been created in His likeness, we're personal, relational, and communicative beings. The issue is not whether we'll communicate, but how effectively we will do it. Your identity in Christ is the most important key to Supernatural selling and living. After that, however, our ability to communicate and connect when we do is vitally important. Effective and persuasive communication always develops trust.

If trust is missing in the interview process, then value, importance, and urgency are drastically diminished until it becomes an uphill battle. Trust is the common denominator to all successful interviews and how we turn someone we have met for the first time into a long-term customer.

It's beginning with the end in mind.

Proverbs talks about every aspect of communication. From the tone of our voice, to the skill necessary to influence, to having conviction in what we say, to learning the importance of listening, to how we frame what we say, and even how to paint pictures with our words.

This is invaluable information since what makes the most difference in our results is not just what we say but how we say it and dig a little deeper, why we say it. The "why" is the weight of our words that creates the greatest level of trust. Some people think trust cannot be seen, that it sort of is or isn't. Stephen Covey in his book, "The Speed of Trust; The One Thing That Changes Everything", explains that the fact is, trust is visible, quantitative, and measurable.

Watch people's body language when you connect and trust is developed. More importantly, watch the results: They will buy more often, increase their level of investment, and refer you to others.

In every interview where resistance is felt, the wall we encounter is distrust.

We can be precise and on script but if our communication doesn't develop trust, the prospect will misinterpret and discount what we say.

In high-trust interviews, we might not say everything correctly, but the customer gets what we're saying.

Developing trust is not a slow process.

The fact is, nothing is as fast as the speed of trust.

We need to know this because, in a relatively short period of time, you're going to have someone, pay hundreds to thousands of dollars in what you are offering. The amount they spend isn't the primary factor. Trust is.

Many believe that the consumer has gotten more sophisticated. I would say they have become more distrustful.

Here is how we develop trust in terms of 3C's.

First: Caring. We've all heard that people don't care what you know until they know that you care.

The core of this concept is all about proactive listening. Entering into our customer's world and getting on the same side of the desk is huge when it comes to developing trust.

The deeper we dig into this and allow God to help us to "know" the customer, the more SUPERnatural the results.

One of the most powerful Scriptures in this regard is found in Philippians 2:3-4. It talks about doing nothing with selfish motives, and in verse 4, "Let each of you look out not only for his own interests, but the interests of others!" This one verse gave me clarity in the cause I have every day. It has turned what I do into a calling. I am focused more on what's important to the customer than the commission.

The greatest misconception about sales is that it's about getting something from others. Sales at its SUPERnatural best and purest form is about giving to others. If we just learn skills and techniques and lose sight of this, we've lost sight of what in reality, causes us to have greater results in less time.

This is a powerful Golden Rule Principle:

There are only so many reasons a person buys from you as it relates to your product or service. There are only so many objections to them doing so. Have you written down, why the customer buys and why they might not? If you're caught flat footed in this regard, you won't get results. You owe it to your customer to be professional, at the same time passionate and both come from being prepared.

As an exercise, develop a "Speed of Trust" Template: Write down:

1. What motivates your customer to buy? (i.e. pocketbook, or personal: how it affects family, business, etc.)
2. What needs does your product or service meet?
3. What is your competitive advantage?

As you think about the possible objections, ask your associates who are proven top producers, what they say and, more importantly, ask the Lord about what to say. When you invite Him into the process, you will be amazed at the insight He will give you. Then, with an understanding of who the potential customer is, take time to practice, drill, and rehearse the answer so you're prepared with what to say, and more importantly, know and have a conviction about "why" you're saying it. If you treat your profession as a hobby and not a profession, you will have to be satisfied with average to below average earnings. You probably will find yourself frustrated and looking for greener pastures. The problem is, you are taking you with you! Here's the good news: Right now, where you are, it is a choice! You can, on purpose, become so developed in this process, that you will be connecting with customers at the heart level, developing lasting relationships and enjoying a long-term satisfying career.

If we haven't listened, what we say will fall on deaf ears. When I train, I tell people that this process and preparation begins *before* you're in front of anyone. Think about what you say and why. I have a speed of trust template that allows me to remember why what I'm saying is important.

I keep on the front what may be important to them on the front burner of my heart. Instead of reaching for words in the moment, I'm confident in what I'm saying. I have seen this turn what looked like an obstacle to buying into a compelling reason to buy! Most objections are plausible and powerful reasons to proceed, if we are prepared and truly know what we offer is of value to the customer.

Take a walk in their shoes!

People want to be heard, not ignored or lip service. They need to know that we get them. When we purposefully and consistently take a walk in their shoes, they will know we do! We enter their circle of trust and speak in such a way that resonates and doesn't alienate. Proverbs 15:2 says the tongue of the wise makes knowledge acceptable. This occurs when that knowledge relates to what's important to them and can only be discovered when we're quick to hear and not quick to speak. If we're not tuned in, they'll be tuned out. In his famous prayer, St. Francis asked God to help him to "Seek first to understand, then to be understood." This principle is a key to communication that develops trust. In **Proverbs 18:13**, the Message Bible says that answering before listening is both stupid and rude. Pretty blunt but right on.

Earlier in this same chapter verse 2 the NLT says, "A fool finds no pleasure in understanding but delights in airing his own opinions."

Second "C": Competence. People tend to trust us when we're competent and distrust us when we're not.

We practice, drill, and rehearse so we have the words on time, because if we don't, we lower the value, importance, and urgency of the interview and raise the level of distrust. Proverbs 16:23: The heart of the wise teaches his mouth and adds persuasiveness to his lips. I might add, even though we take time to prepare, we also, trust God to give us what to say in the moment when we don't know what to say. I have found that I can draw from my heart what I didn't know in my head and it will be exactly what they needed to hear. God will give you wisdom. All you have to do is ask!

The third "C" is for **Conviction**. People hear how we say what we say and know when our "why" is big enough. It's important not just to have the words on time but to know why those words are meaningful to the customer. Just like the concept of "caring", one of the best ways to add persuasiveness to our lips is not just to practice the words, but to think about who the customer is and what motivates him to buy, which develops our conviction.

Someone said the last 4 letters of enthusiasm, "iasm", stand for I am sold myself! People are moved by what sincerely moves us.

We should have plausible and powerful reasons for people to buy what we offer, but none of it works if we don't communicate with conviction. If what you offer can't be sold with conviction, find something that can because when you do, the SUPERnatural becomes natural because you are conveying from the heart what you offer.

This well of conviction doesn't have a bottom to it, and puts us in a position of influence to a greater degree than we could have imagined because we're communicating with passion and professionalism. It's the primary reason people who say the same thing get vastly different results. When caring, competence, and conviction are present, so too, is a high level of trust and a high level of results.

This changes the quantity of interviews to quality interviews and how many of you know, if you do enough, and you do it correctly, you'll have success on purpose? The more proficient you get at this, the more you will do in less time. The words you speak will carry a level of influence that goes well beyond words on a script.

Chapter 23

Neuro-Linguistic Programming: The Speed of Rapport

There is a lot of research being done in what is called Neuro-Linguistic Programming (NLP).

NLP is comprised of three key components of human communication: Neuro relates to the mind, linguistics to the language, and programming is the way we process what we're hearing and how we like to be heard. I found, it took a couple of weeks to learn how to pick up on the communication styles of potential customers. At the same time, it is now an integral part of how I relate because it has dramatically increased my results and the results of those I have trained.

Sales at its best has to do with connecting. We're often impressed with people who can speak several languages. I think it's more important if a person can hear and really connect in one.

We do business at the "speed of trust." Digging into this topic a little more, we find that we do business at the Speed of Rapport, which to do well, trust is a must.

Taking a walk in the customer's shoes, knowing what to say and why we say it relative to their needs and interests is vitally important. These are foundational steps of how we build a bridge and not fortify the wall of distrust.

In this regard, communication that builds trust is more than lip service and more than technique. Sincerity is powerful. It positions you on the same side of the desk as your customer where you experience higher levels of communication and effectiveness. Value, importance and urgency increase as we truly connect.

At the same time, not everyone is programmed the same way to hear our message or our heart.

This is where it gets interesting. People connect differently and we can develop rapport rapidly if we read them accurately.

Let me explain. According to NLP, there are three basic ways people connect when they communicate. These numbers are approximate, but:

Twenty-five percent are auditory: In other words, they are listening carefully to our words and they want us to hear their words.

Thirty-five percent are visual: They want us to "see" what they're saying and in turn they process best when they can "see" what we're saying.

Approximately forty percent are kinesthetic: They want to "feel" what they're saying and relate best when they can "feel" what we're saying.

Note: Everyone can communicate using all three ways, but we connect when we discover how they predominately hear.

For us to broaden our influence, and increase our results, we've got to listen, ask questions and speak the way they best hear us.

People want to do business with people most like themselves. They may not put their finger on why, but they know when they have connected with you or not. You should, too. This takes mirroring your customer to another level. Again, this is not meant to be a technique to get your product into their hands and their dollars into your pocket. It is to add value by going the extra mile in connecting, and when you focus on that, the whole process will be profitable and a win-win for your customer and you.

The Importance of questions: Imagine a thermometer near your potential customer. They're at thirty-two degrees (icy cold) and in order to do business with them, they need to be at eighty degrees. When you are talking, there's slow, imperceptible movement on the thermometer. However, when you ask the right questions and listen, the mercury's movement is noticeable. The problem with listening is, many people think they are listening and they are not. They're just reloading.

Connecting takes place at deeper and more meaningful levels when you ask questions, listen and speak in the way they predominantly communicate. Besides that, you won't lose opportunities through over-qualifying. There are times when you think people are not interested when in fact, they are just tracking differently. We need to be more in touch with the way they hear us if we want greater results. When you begin to understand this principle, you will amp up your conviction because you will know you are speaking their language.

1. Auditory Communicators, NLP Questions: Because they grasp concepts through *words,* here are some questions you can ask:

-Tell me more

-What are your thoughts?

-What are you thinking?

Responses to an Auditory:

-I hear what you're saying.

-That makes sense.

-I understand.

Body Language of an Auditory:

-They are the least demonstrative (i.e. they don't have a lot of hand motions)

-They may lean in with their ear: Don't get thrown by this especially if you are giving a visual presentation. Just know they are tracking with you and emphasize your words. When they speak, lean in with your ear to focus on what they are saying. This relates to them more than you know.

To know whether a person is an auditory learner, listen for cues in what they say, such as:

-*That sounds good to me!*

-*I hear what you're saying.*

-*That's makes sense to me.*

Note: Auditory learners want you to get to the verbal point.

They are not touchy-feely type people. Painting word pictures as you would with a visual or a kinesthetic, will not connect with them at their heart level. They are listening to your words.

They may seem uninterested and maybe some are, but often they're following you and if you pick up on it, you can emphasize words with rate, pace, and intonation.

2. Visual Communicators, NLP Questions: Because they want to see what you are saying and they want you to see what they are saying. Questions that resonate with a visual include:

-How do you see it?

-What kind of picture does that paint for you?

-Imagine (insert a word picture)

-What does that look like to you?

Responses to a Visual:

-I see what you mean.

-I can see that.

-I can picture what you're saying.

Body Language of a Visual:

-They are animated and demonstrative, (i.e. use their hands to make a point, etc.)

To know whether a person is a visual learner, listen and watch for cues in what they say, such as:

-They paint word pictures and are demonstrative with their hands.

-I see it this way.

-I look at it this way.

-I imagine it this way

Note: Pictures, while they do not relate well to an auditory, put you on the same side of the desk as a visual. Pictures paint a thousand words to them. Knowing this, your presentation should include visuals that help them see what you are saying. Your body language should be animated as well.

3. Kinesthetic Communicators, NLP Questions

-How do you feel about that?

-What does that make you feel like?

Responses to a Kinesthetic:

-I can feel what you're saying.

-I feel that.

-What you said, touched me.

Body Language of a Kinesthetic:

They don't use as much body language as a visual, but they can. However, they are more emotional.

To know whether a person is a Kinesthetic learner, listen for cues in what they say, such as:

-They, too can paint word pictures but their language is about feeling, i.e. I feel like, or this is how it makes me feel. Depending on what you're offering, I've seen them tear up.

-I've felt this way...

-My gut tells me...

Note: A Kinesthetic wants to feel what you are saying so if you have anything they can touch, feel, etc. or something that is hands on so they can experience the product, they will connect with to a greater degree than if you just told them or painted a word picture.

Here are some examples of how I've used NLP in the field to relate to customers:

I was in front of an auditory. He wasn't very emotional, nor did he give me much indication that he was interested. I spent less time trying to paint pictures and spoke his language with a conviction that he was listening (even though it didn't look like it.) When he spoke, I leaned in with my ear. I knew I was on his wavelength and he not only bought, but doubled his purchase. This was an important lesson for me because I always thought this kind of communicator was not interested. In times past, I would have "over-qualified" him and went down the road. Now, I'm more aware and I don't miss the opportunity to connect with these types of communicators.

At another time, I was giving a presentation to partners. As I have gotten better at this, I am now able to pick up on things quicker. One was an auditory, the other was a visual. As I painted pictures to the visual, I noticed the auditory gentlemen was drifting. I then simply asked him his thoughts and he became re-engaged. The result, both agreed and bought.

Another example of this happened when I made a presentation to an all-in Kinesthetic. She wanted me to feel what she was saying. I kept relating to her on her level by saying, I feel what you're saying. I appreciate your passion about this, etc. Then I had her use a mobile app we offered and walked her through the process. The truth is, my presentation was not that stellar but my level of connecting with her was. She knew I was speaking her language and she invested a substantial amount.

The importance of understanding this is that you ask questions that resonate, make statements that are couched in terms that relate with the customer. While you are doing this, you will find you are listening more intently, and more importantly, you will know what you are saying is resonating. It makes the whole sales process easier because true rapport has been developed on a deeper level.

In John Maxwell's book, "Everyone Communicates, Few Connect", He outlines the litmus test for high-level rapport by asking the question:

How do I know I've connected? You will notice:

-**UNSOLICITED APPRECIATION:** (i.e. Keep up the good work, etc.)

- **UNSOLICITED OPENNESS:** Depth of conversation

- **INCREASED CONVERSATION**, Less pulling teeth, more of a flow

- **ENJOYABLE EXPERIENCE:** They are buying, not being sold

- **EMOTIONAL BOND:** Deeper level of connecting

- **POSITIVE ENERGY OF A WIN-WIN INTERACTION:** They've heard your heart and you've heard theirs

-**GROWING SYNERGY THAT IS BEYOND HOW WELL YOU GAVE THE PRESENTATION:** You will sense, even if you didn't give a stellar presentation, that rapport carried the day.

-THEY SENSE YOU ARE ON THE GIVE AND THEIR WALLS ARE DOWN SO THEY CAN RECEIVE

Summary:

1. Listen for how they speak; locate how you need to relate to them.

2. Let your questions, statements, and even the way you listen be in that mode.

3. Review results and see if you're connecting!

God is a stickler for motives. We all have a degree of self-interest, but God's way is to be love-centered. Focus on the needs, wants, and interests of others first. Going the extra mile by taking a walk in their shoes and relating to them at the heart level is the Golden Rule of **SUPERNATURAL** selling!

Prayer to Receive Christ/Where the SUPERnatural BEGINS

Salvation is a gift we receive in Christ.

God loves us as we are, not as we should be. We grow by learning to trust God to help us change in our thinking and our actions. That's the journey we're on

God went to great lengths to provide salvation.

John 3:16

"For God so loved the world, that He gave His only begotten Son, that whoever believes in Him shall not perish, but have eternal life."

How can you receive God's free gift of love and eternal life?

Romans 10:9 "If you confess with your mouth Jesus as Lord, and believe in your heart that God raised Him from the dead, you will be saved!"

A person receives God's free gift of love and life by placing faith in Jesus Christ. To believe is simply to take God at His word. With our heart we believe that Jesus is God's Son who died for our sin on the cross and arose from the grave to live in us as Savior and Lord.

Romans 10:13

"For Whoever will call on the name of the Lord will be saved."

This has nothing to do with feelings. It is by faith!

To call means simply to ask. The verse does not require one to know more... do better... clean up one's life... or in any way try to add to what Jesus has done for us. You may say, that's too easy, but the reality is, it's humbling, but it's true.

The journey to a SUPERNATURAL life, begins with a simple prayer according to His Word like this:

"Father, I confess that I'm a sinner, and I'm sorry. I need a Savior. Your Word says, Jesus died on the cross, three days later He arose again, and that if I receive and trust Him, I will be saved. I ask You, Lord Jesus, to forgive my sin and come into my heart. I trust you as my Savior and receive you as my Lord. Thank you, Jesus, for saving me."

Did you say this prayer and mean it from your heart? Here's God's promise: **When anyone calls on the Lord in this manner, they are saved. You have God's word on it.**

Friend, it's that simple. This is the first day of your forever life and the first day for you to experience His Super on your natural for every area of your life.

I know you're going to want to tell someone about your experience in accepting Christ or you might have a question. Feel free to write me:

danrmaclean@gmail.com.

About the Author:

Dan Maclean

For over 20 years, Dan Maclean has been a national sales trainer, coach, and mentor, business owner and author. He has been blessed to train and develop top sales producers all across the country, not from a distance or in theory, but in the field where the rubber meets the road and results are expected.

Dan has been married close to 40 years, to Judi, and has 2 daughters, Nicole and Dara. He has seen firsthand how the concepts found in this book discovered in "The Book" will help you win in your career and succeed in life.

Dan teaches the connection between God and work to develop people who are Professional, Passionate and Purposeful. The original word for sales meant "to give!"

Dan believes the Sales Profession is a "high" calling when this "Golden Rule" principle becomes the core conviction. He exemplifies the fact that if you have your head and heart in whatever you're called to do, you can expect powerful results!

Dan, through wisdom found in the Word of God, has introduced and taught a results oriented "On Purpose" system which has consistently produced top achievers, high dollar earners and long term careers.

He teaches how to process through a different paradigm that is not just about being the best you can be or the worst you've been, for that matter. Both are just different size boxes. The SUPERnatural Salesperson is part of a journey to discover that there are greater levels of passion, purpose and power available if we learn to do it God's way.

Dan has experienced, first hand, that when professional sales people learn how to replace self-confidence with a confidence in God, they discover they can do more than they can do and have a satisfying, meaningful career in the process. Dan teaches that our success DNA is realized when we grasp the fact that we are God made and not self-made and that the greatest journey we can embark in any endeavor of life is to know Him and know His ways.

Know Him, we'll know what, why and how! This changes everything.

Dan Maclean: Contact Information

SUPERnatural Salesperson: The GOD Factor in Sales may be ordered in bulk or individually for churches, company trainings, study groups or personal use.

Contact the author, Dan Maclean, by mail, telephone or email:

Dan Maclean

8101 Boat Club Dr. #1277

Fort Worth, TX 76179

Phone: (817) 680-7492

Email: danrmaclean@gmail.com